Scrumptious Thursday

CROSSWORDS

Edited by
PETER GORDON

STERLING

New York / London
www.sterlingpublishing.com

The puzzles in this book originally appeared on Thursdays in
The New York Sun from March 3, 2005, to July 20, 2006,
and are also reprinted in "The New York Sun Crosswords" series,
published by Sterling Publishing Co., Inc.

2   4   6   8   10   9   7   5   3   1

Published by Sterling Publishing Co., Inc.
387 Park Avenue South, New York, NY 10016
© 2008 by Sterling Publishing Co., Inc.
Distributed in Canada by Sterling Publishing
c/o Canadian Manda Group, 165 Dufferin Street
Toronto, Ontario, Canada M6K 3H6
Distributed in the United Kingdom by GMC Distribution Services
Castle Place, 166 High Street, Lewes, East Sussex, England BN7 1XU
Distributed in Australia by Capricorn Link (Australia) Pty. Ltd.
P.O. Box 704, Windsor, NSW 2756, Australia

Sterling ISBN-13: 978-1-4027-5335-0
ISBN-10: 1-4027-5335-7

For information about custom editions, special sales, premium and
corporate purchases, please contact Sterling Special Sales
Department at 800-805-5489 or specialsales@sterlingpublishing.com.

CONTENTS

INTRODUCTION

The 72 puzzles in this book are manna for the crossword gourmand. They are taken from Thursday newspapers, which means they are quite challenging. Just over half of them have themes, and many of those themes involve toothsome twists. The themeless puzzles have juicy long entries and savory clues meant to trip you up.

If you find yourself with a bitter taste in your mouth because you can't finish these puzzles, try "Tasty Tuesday Crosswords" or "Delicious Wednesday Crosswords" instead. But if you make it through all 72 and want to try ones with even more spice, then be sure to pick up "Flavorful Friday Crosswords."

—Peter Gordon

THEMELESS 1

BY ALAN OLSCHWANG

ACROSS
1 Surfing need
11 Golfer Dutra who won the 1934 U.S. Open
15 Sydney has a famous one
16 Biblical miracle site
17 Businesslike
18 Harshly reprimand, with "out"
19 Retirement's beginning
20 Like some scholars
22 ___ Cats ("Rock This Town" group)
25 Where the action is
26 Word with tennis or shoe
30 "Beautiful Goodbye" singer Jennifer
32 Robot drama
33 Water polo, etc.
35 Thingamajig

37 Cultivate
38 Musical hold
39 Frolic
40 Adorned, in a way
41 It ends in septembre
42 Secluded roads
44 Costner role of 1987
45 "Same here"
47 Relating to the last division of the small intestine
49 Do a farming job
51 Exclamation of grief
55 Have ___ (know somebody)
56 Early calculators
60 Umpteen

61 Police department officer
62 Frog spit, e.g.
63 Seconds

DOWN
1 Ended up up
2 Collection of poems
3 De ___ esse (provisionally, in law)
4 Bones of fiction
5 Hindu princesses
6 Fruitangy ___ (Quaker cereal)
7 Exclamation of grief
8 Vacationers' souvenirs, perhaps

9 Contents of "The Federalist"
10 Film unit
11 Befall
12 County in Alabama, Mississippi, and Tennessee
13 Slyly suggests
14 Working-class family men, in political-speak
21 Noble estates
23 XXX
24 Triathlon, e.g.
26 Performing arts center offering
27 Like algebra
28 Horse's activity in dressage

29 Bruce Lee's role in "The Green Hornet"
31 Texas city that's the setting for the film "Friday Night Lights"
34 Tasty flatfish
36 Bodement
38 She was Bonnie to Warren's Clyde
40 Counts
43 Basketball Hall of Famer Reed
46 Skater Harding
48 Proofreading symbol
50 Cuba, por ejemplo
52 Roman goddess of the moon
53 "American Beauty" screenwriter Ball
54 Enraptured
57 Result of mixing gas and alcohol?
58 UFO crew
59 A and B, in D.C.

ANSWER, PAGE 79

TURNING STATE'S EVIDENCE

BY JOE DIPIETRO

ACROSS

1 1980 Boston Marathon "winner" Rosie
5 Wrongs
10 Dearth
14 "The Dark at the Top of the Stairs" playwright
15 Island north of Venezuela's Paraguaná Peninsula
16 Willing partner?
17 One who handles a scene with poise?
20 Casually pass
21 Golfer's accessory
22 Super Bowl in which Joe Namath was the MVP
23 "Whatcha waitin' for?"
25 Obliged to pay actor Leonard?
33 Cutting room?
34 "Dynasty" actress
35 "... shall live?" reply
36 Analogous
37 A bit bonkers
38 Handle
39 Greenish parrot
40 Senator's rival
41 Tally mark
42 Long range charity dinners?
45 Not quite closed
46 Pink-slip
47 Not included
50 Garage band recording
55 Boiled Bean snapped?
58 TV teacher of Vinnie, Arnold, Juan, and Freddie
59 Business person
60 Small screen honor
61 Checked out
62 Sanctify
63 Supreme being?

DOWN

1 Frees (of)
2 Co-op division
3 Lab worker with a hunch
4 Get closer to
5 Onetime Dey costar
6 Shatt-al-___ (river of Iraq)
7 40th anniversary gift
8 Kellogg School deg.
9 Utah's La ___ Mountains
10 Cause of odd weather
11 Fundamentals
12 Dog in the sitcom "The People's Choice"
13 Six-time loser for Best Actress
18 Adjust, in a way
19 Swears
23 Let in for free
24 "Goodness gracious!"
25 City east of Kobe
26 Don't leave out?
27 Old war story
28 Weather map line
29 Language that gave us the word "kiwi"
30 Bellyband
31 Ukase
32 Juniors' juniors, for short
37 Artie was her first ex
38 Aggressively enterprising person
40 White's partner
41 Time's 1971 Man of the Year
43 Part of ERA
44 Rats, often
47 Margin
48 With 49-Down, container of high-energy electrons
49 See 48-Down
50 Newton fraction
51 They might be found in woolly cotes
52 Shells, e.g.
53 Actress Grier and others
54 "Grand" brand of ice cream
56 Mug
57 Screech producer

ANSWER, PAGE 80

8

MARCH MADNESS

BY CHARLES E. GERSCH

ACROSS

1 Noted b-baller
5 Position without much room for advancement
10 Spurt
13 Locale of Makapuu Lighthouse
14 Bakery lure
15 Western tribe
16 National League stadium
17 Mel's "Lethal Weapon" costar
18 Ardent
19 Kids' alphabet game opener
22 Sugar servings
23 Word with eye or jaw
24 Joe ___ (former cigarette mascot)
27 One in a fright wig
29 Feeling of reverence
30 With 39-Across, a book by 42-Across (and the key to this puzzle's theme)
34 Like some radios
37 Stadium section
39 See 30-Across
40 Past time
41 Upbraid

42 See 30-Across
44 Dobbin's driblet
45 Charter
47 Some reunion attendees
49 Keats, for one
51 They can be split in blackjack
54 Major corporation that was headquartered in Pennsylvania
59 Mimic
60 Tale tail, sometimes
61 Setting of the opening scene of "Saving Private Ryan"
63 Variety show act
64 Pale yellow

65 Movie shot
66 Clear button on computer calculators
67 Tandem twosomes
68 1976 Gregory Peck film, with "The"

DOWN

1 Message that may be written in large letters
2 "That's a laugh!"
3 Attention-getter noise
4 "Worth Fighting For" author
5 Working girl's boss
6 Restrict

7 Desmond and Molly's last name in "Ob-La-Di, Ob-La-Da"
8 Book of Mormon book
9 Hound's howls
10 Io, e.g.
11 Heroic poems
12 Nautical almanac topics
15 Corridor
20 Having no force
21 Erenow
24 Dogie, e.g.
25 No-show GI
26 Like Stonehenge
27 Piscine "Pinocchio" character
28 Spotted

31 "___ the One" (Elvis Presley hit on the flip side of "Heartbreak Hotel")
32 Lacquered metalware
33 HBO competitor
35 Brothers' home, briefly
36 National League team
38 Range of vision
43 Decorate gaudily, with "up"
46 Surrounder of the Bahamas: Abbr.
48 Comfortable with
49 Not merely tubby
50 Flattens
51 Risk
52 Achieve a magician's goal
53 Man and others
55 Actress Watson of the "Harry Potter" movies
56 The Hitler Diaries, e.g.
57 Town about 10 miles from Amsterdam
58 Camp sight
62 1,000 rin

ANSWER, PAGE 82

THEMELESS 2

BY ADAM COHEN

ACROSS

1 Company listed on the Australian stock exchange
7 Province that borders Málaga
14 2002 Atom Egoyan movie set in Armenia
15 Mobs
16 Brewer of music
17 Knicks' bricks
18 ___ Arundel (Maryland county)
19 Kvetch
21 "Marsupial ___" (John Lithgow children's book)
22 Last Soviet first lady
24 Beams
25 Madonna was on its first cover in May 1985
26 "The Heart ___ Lonely Hunter"
27 '40s All-Star shortstop Stephens
29 Lao-tzu adherent
31 One side in eightball
33 Ceremonial staffs
34 Caractacus Potts portrayer on film
36 Piano's opposite
38 "Roger ___ Book of Film"
39 "Aunt Jo's Scrap-Bag" writer
41 Tennis player Silvia Farina ___
42 Sushi bar quaff
45 Actress Young
46 Sabra's airline
48 Old Testament book after Micah
50 Vacation rental?
51 Longtime San Francisco Examiner publisher
53 Alternative to Mega Bloks
54 Fearless
56 Saws
58 Villain, at times
59 Hard cheese
60 Hue named for a terrestrial planet
61 Saint of France?

DOWN

1 Doha denizen
2 Diamonds and rings
3 Magical land created by C.S. Lewis
4 They're often clear-cut
5 Small batteries
6 Postpone
7 Full of dirt
8 Least prevalent
9 Truncated wd.
10 Org. for shooters
11 Condiment from the myrtle family
12 "Fatso" star
13 Yeses
17 Swimming gold medalist at Athens
20 Show up
23 Long-legged bird
25 Enjoys a long bath
28 Yellowstone sight
30 "The Kitchen God's Wife" author
31 Be ready for, as a fat pitch
32 Fishhook attachments
34 Noah Wyle's "ER" role
35 Wash'n ___ (towelette brand)
36 Mussolini's movement
37 1992 David Mamet play
40 Lodging with a reservation
42 Retailer based in San Francisco
43 University of Oregon home
44 "In the Land of Israel" author
47 Scottish landowner
49 National competitor
51 Fräulein's fiancé
52 Bakery offering
55 ___ ipsa loquitur
57 Caméra ___ (Cannes prize)

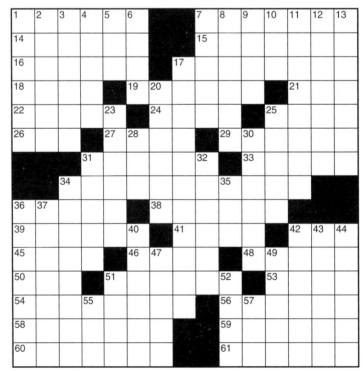

ANSWER, PAGE 84

THE LAST GOODBYE

BY PAULA GAMACHE

ACROSS

1 "8 Simple Rules" airer
4 Quite a stretch
7 Brown of publishing
11 Fan sound
12 TV sked letters
13 Supervise
17 Do the wrong thing
18 Falsetto
20 Santa ___ (California racetrack)
22 Loopy Soupy
23 Sessanta minuti
24 Like adobe bricks
26 Stiffly formal
27 Frist's predecessor
29 Queue following R
30 Rainwear brand
31 A ___ (deductive)
33 Macaulay Culkin, to Bonnie Bedelia
35 Stood out
36 Banned apple spray
37 Pop trio from Oslo with the hit "Take On Me"
40 Objectivist philosopher Rand

41 Coal deposit
43 Pack members
45 Zapata's z's
47 Jazz players, e.g.
48 Paintball sound
50 S&L portfolio holding
52 Nixon of the Red Sox
53 Stuff with stuff
54 Ivory tower setting
56 Emeritus: Abbr.
57 Silver, in Sevilla
58 The Dow, for one
61 Deadly defoliant
64 ThinkCentre maker

65 One of a series of recurring actions
66 JFK, once
67 Mined matter
68 Spare hair
69 Ring stat
70 Sequel title starter

DOWN

1 Quarter
2 Animal house
3 "Heathers" costar
4 "___ Frome"
5 Sake server's sash
6 Plagues
7 Involving important people, as a meeting

8 Like Columbia's walls
9 Crosse pieces
10 Projectile's path
14 Some receivers
15 Paranormal
16 Cheeseboard selections
19 "Problem-free philosophy" from "The Lion King"
21 Give a one-on-one lesson to
25 Backs of hits
26 The Baltimore Ravens are named in his honor

27 Babe Zaharias was a founding member of it: Abbr.
28 French runway locale
30 Pulsate
32 Tripmeter button
34 Oklahoma Indian
38 One who is worshiped
39 Aide: Abbr.
42 They're often swiped
44 Exempli gratia, e.g.
46 "___ Charlotte Simmons" (Tom Wolfe novel)
48 Neck, slangily
49 Chunky Garden pasta sauce brand
51 Hanseatic League city
54 Take-___ (portable)
55 Appearances
57 Spitting sound
59 The Aragón is one of its tributaries
60 Cyclops, Wolverine, et al.
62 First word of "Richard III"
63 Prefix with politics

ANSWER, PAGE 86

ONE MAN OUT

BY JOHN MINARCIK AND CRAIG KASPER

ACROSS

1 See 37-Across and 56-Across
6 Tosses in
10 FIRST BASEMAN
13 Boston Patriots running back Jim
14 25 décembre
15 It might be divided into eras
16 Italian dialect
18 PITCHER
20 Choose, with "for"
21 Uninterrupted sequence
23 Dome-topped building
24 SECOND BASEMAN
26 Captures
28 Future monarch, perhaps
29 Approaching
30 Orange ghost in Ms. Pac-Man
31 Like prison windows
33 Opposite of alt
34 Muffler
36 Comment from a snake
37 SHORTSTOP, after 1-Across
41 Direction prefix
44 Ukes are played at them
45 Org. whose logo includes an eagle holding a balance
48 Spear
50 Piece of lawn
52 Copper
54 Bridge
55 "Kilroy was ___"
56 THIRD BASEMAN, after 1-Across
57 Having a will
60 Potato chip flavor, for short
62 Bowl over
63 Topic of a classic 1940s comedy routine, and the inspiration of this puzzle
65 ___ l'oeil
67 "Spider-Man 2" villain Doc ___
68 National, once
69 Simple Halloween costume
70 LEFT FIELDER
71 Enumerate
72 CATCHER

DOWN

1 Back from a trip
2 French king's eldest son
3 Like a curtain call
4 Letters on the Enterprise
5 Glum drop
6 Orkin target
7 "Love Me Two Times" group, with "the"
8 Sale item, often
9 Narrow opening
10 Nobelists Heisenberg and Forssmann
11 Sweats with tops
12 Straight ahead
17 Letters on dreidels
19 German flower
22 Butterflies and then some
25 Shark's muscle, say
27 CENTER FIELDER
31 Protector of a car's front end
32 Where to go to go to Togo: Abbr.
35 Accumulate on a surface, as a dissolved substance
38 Home to DePaul U.
39 Saturn offering
40 Small groove
41 Fog bank phenomenon
42 Challenge the credibility of
43 Fischer beat him in Reykjavik
46 Changed the title of
47 Chinese food veggie
49 Word on a Caribbean Stud Poker table
51 It's outstanding
53 Granny's pet, in cartoons
55 Is somewhat effective
58 First homicide victim
59 Hack
61 Queue before U
64 Fortune
66 Discoverer's shout

ANSWER, PAGE 88

THEMELESS 3

BY OGDEN PORTER

ACROSS

1 Haglike
7 Powerful weapons
13 Development time
15 Gallimaufry
16 Decisive defeat
18 Sister of Stheno and Euryale
19 Baseball feature
20 It might be unhooked while hooking up
22 Hot
23 "Industry" for Utah, e.g.
26 Loose end?
27 Interjection of disapproval
28 Certain Protestant
30 Page with think pieces
32 "Il ___ tesoro" ("Don Giovanni" aria)
33 Four-time champion of the Australian Open
37 Drive
39 XLV × IX
41 City north of Lake Nasser

42 Engagement agreement
44 Masseuse's supply
46 Hashish source
47 Tiger Mountain's locale
50 Rhea's cousin
51 "Welcome to the next level" sloganeer
54 Four-book series by Paul Scott, with "The"
56 Plant with both disk and ray flowers
58 Little, in Lille
59 City in Deutschland
60 Brawl souvenir

62 Rich
65 V.P. born in D.C.
66 Be postponed
67 One who squirrels things away
68 R&B singer with the hit "Nobody Else"

DOWN

1 Thrill
2 Dazed
3 Two-person conversation
4 Swindle
5 Spam source
6 Ernest's successor as Best Actor
7 Sleeve

8 Singer with the hit album "Diamonds & Rust"
9 "The Germ" poet
10 Timid person
11 Some sculptures
12 Corset, to a Brit
14 Operating automatically
17 Kapparah ceremony participant
21 Polished off
23 Long-running Off-Broadway show featuring unusual percussion instruments
24 Silent

25 ___ serrata (retina part)
29 Lord, in Turkish
31 The Colorado Rockies' first manager
34 Anita Baker's first hit
35 Director of "Road to Perdition"
36 Opinion
38 It premiered in Prague in 1921
40 Shortstop Omar who won nine straight Gold Glove Awards
43 ___ supuesto (of course, in Spanish)
45 Apt name for a restroom attendant
48 Downy surface
49 A shooting star
51 Conversation pit pieces
52 Ennoble
53 Start
55 Turbine part
57 Limerick's land
61 For each one
63 Plastered
64 Smithsonite, e.g.

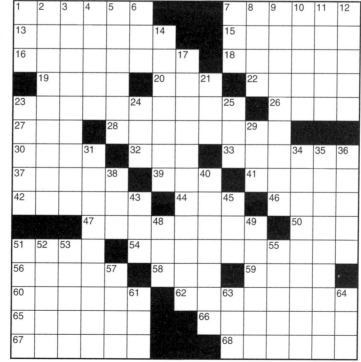

ANSWER, PAGE 90

13

SET 'EM UP

BY GARY STEINMEHL

ACROSS
1 Treasure
4 Sportsmanship Award org.
8 Mr. Spock's specialty
13 Ike's command
14 Astringent substance
15 Drastically affect
16 Tropical tuber
18 Knob
19 Sideshow performers
20 1957 and 1958 Wimbledon and U.S. Open winner
23 Link
24 Physical responses
25 Tommy James and the Shondells hit
28 Song featured in the movie "You Were Never Lovelier"
33 Juillet follower
34 Grow weary
35 2002 Jennifer Lopez movie
42 Woody offspring at Woodstock
43 Prevarications
44 "Shallow Hal" costar
51 Tenn. neighbor
52 Run up a tab
53 Chair man?
55 Author of "The Jury" and "The Arraignment"
59 Less-traveled road
62 Spirited self-assurance
63 Popeyed
64 Baseball commissioner Kuhn
65 Knock down
66 Goaltending site
67 Bee product
68 Large number
69 Special time

DOWN
1 Intimate
2 Bibliography phrase
3 Post-___
4 1880 Émile Zola novel
5 Plumbing problem
6 Autobahn auto
7 Tiny eukaryotes
8 Frequent Karloff costar
9 Unfolded
10 "Fancy that!"
11 Cuttlefish ejection
12 They earn int.
17 Louisville's river
21 Zhou ___
22 Call for quiet
25 Foul mood
26 Sister of Poseidon
27 Tree of knowledge locale
29 Juan or Carlos
30 Giant word
31 Dickens title starter
32 Six-time N.L. home run leader
35 Goya subject
36 Asia's ___ Sea
37 Character who says "Play it, Sam"
38 "Yabba dabba ___!"
39 Shoot down
40 "Hath ___ sister?": Shakespeare
41 Santa portrayer in "Elf"
45 Reply to "Is it ready?"
46 Slack-jawed feeling
47 Hand brakes, e.g.
48 Information
49 An American in Paris, maybe
50 Manet contemporary
54 Fraternity letter
55 Travel in a windjammer
56 Its fleet is made up entirely of Boeings
57 Puzzle on a place mat
58 From scratch
59 Chicken preparation, for short
60 What U sometimes means
61 It ended La Belle Époque: Abbr.

ANSWER, PAGE 92

THEMELESS 4

BY EDGAR FONTAINE

ACROSS
1 They have keys
5 "What am I, chopped liver?!"
9 Disguised, for short
14 Parrots
15 Playboy's bunny, e.g.
16 Kind of battery
17 Wacky entertainer born Scott Thompson
19 "The Rules of Engagement" novelist Brookner
20 Behave badly, with "out"
21 Tabby treater
22 Medical diagnostic test
23 Vodka cocktail
27 Malagueño's title
28 Feel small
32 Pass catchers
34 Oscilloscope part: Abbr.
35 Finger, in a way

36 Cell user's question
40 Rudiments
41 "Getting ___ of Bradley" (Jennifer Crusie novel)
42 Pledge
43 Took a stab at?
46 Squirrel (away)
49 Make a court judgment
51 Vivacious wit
54 Miler Sebastian
55 Folk singer Williams
56 Storybook ending, perhaps
57 Square dance for four couples

60 Mount Katahdin's locale
61 ___ Laszlo (skin care brand)
62 Savvy duo?
63 Jambeau, e.g.
64 Scatterbrain
65 Go around in circles

DOWN
1 Harsh-voiced parrots
2 Cochise, for one
3 Relevance
4 Chevy model with a retractable hardtop
5 Let out, say
6 Spa
7 I problem?
8 Swabber

9 Source of "let us eat and drink; for tomorrow we shall die"
10 "Tea for Two" musical
11 Illegal block in football
12 They might be rolled
13 "Little Orphan Annie" cartoonist Harold
18 Cook too long
22 Casual eatery
24 Nephew of Uncle Junior
25 Breaks away
26 Song on Bob Dylan's "Desire" album
29 Roughed up

30 "Some mornings it just doesn't seem worth it to gnaw through the leather straps" comedian Philips
31 Drops on the grass
33 Most certain
36 Fleet vehicle?
37 D.A.'s group
38 Charters?
39 Original
44 Carpenter's tool
45 Pour out
47 Went up
48 "The lifeblood of religions," according to André Suarès
50 Product to combat drowsiness
51 Baby Spice's real first name
52 Go parasailing
53 Square-toed
57 Math class abbr.
58 Ocean State sch.
59 Elvis Presley's "___ Lost You"

ANSWER, PAGE 94

15

THREE IN A ROW

BY JAMES S. KAPLAN

ACROSS

1 Grandmother of Jacob and Esau
6 Not Rx
9 Banjoist Fleck, the leader of the Flecktones
13 "A New Argentina" musical
14 "Dedicated to the ___ Love" (hit by the Shirelles)
15 Maneuver named after skater Paulsen
16 Social agency investigator
18 Prix ___
19 "Shame on you!"
20 Eagerly expectant
21 Flowing back
23 Hinder
25 Time's 1954 Man of the Year
26 Put on
27 Usher's workplace
28 St. Nick's holiday
31 "___ She Great" (2000 Bette Midler film)
33 Love, in Lombardy
37 Continue to be
39 Game with half a dozen winning lines found in this puzzle
40 Attach, as a patch
41 Iron anniversary
42 Dink's lack
44 Friend of Sandy Plankton
45 Tied the knot over again
47 1099-___ (annual tax form from the bank)
49 Begin follower
51 Minify
55 Puts one's two cents in
56 Attracted
58 Charlemagne's domain: Abbr.
59 Flower holders
60 Check out ahead of time
63 Counselor on "Star Trek: The Next Generation"
64 ___ de vie (clear brandies)
65 Expeditious
66 Thrilled
67 Social reformer Dorothea
68 Leader of the Merry Pranksters

DOWN

1 Religious denominations
2 Nautical command
3 Hazardous
4 Showed enthusiasm for, with "up"
5 Popular honeymoon destination
6 Peeling spuds, maybe
7 Simple shirt
8 Type of cloud
9 Puzzles
10 Forced absence
11 Acura rival
12 Malcolm's role in "A Clockwork Orange"
14 "... ___ quit!"
17 Comic actress Cheri
22 Grasso and Raines
24 Taxi alternative
25 Copied, in a way
27 Milk of magnesia, e.g.
28 Cross-out marks
29 CCCXXXVII tripled
30 City north of Marseilles
32 Shock source, sometimes
34 Be shy
35 Not ital.
36 Roxy Music's Brian
38 Composition
43 Proctor ___
46 Went up in smoke
48 Aaron Burr's birthplace
49 Future fungus
50 Think of, as a solution
52 Arks and barks, e.g.
53 Hall of Fame catcher Lombardi
54 Wanting
55 Makes a decision
56 Two, in Toulouse
57 Rover's playmate
61 Aishwarya of Bollywood
62 West of Hollywood

ANSWER, PAGE 96

THEMELESS 5

BY MARK DIEHL

ACROSS

1 "A Few Good Men" playwright
12 Player on the tube, maybe
15 Berlitz product
16 BCE part
17 Misty May and Kerri Walsh, in Athens
18 Cry for help
19 Within walking distance
20 Law of Moses
22 Finish
24 Powerful economic coalition
25 Became less painful
27 Commuting option
29 Observance
30 Titillating
32 Racetrack figures
33 Loc. ___
36 Maker of E.L. Fudge cookies
38 Family reunion invitee
39 Short story in James Joyce's "Dubliners"

41 "___ Unplugged" (1999 live album)
43 Brood
44 McSorley's serving
45 A real jerk
48 Brownie mix add-in, often
50 Partner of Roeper
52 Fan of the Alouettes, perhaps
57 "Rendezvous With ___" (Arthur C. Clarke novel)
58 Glass in the radio booth
59 Cruising
61 Digital watch type

62 Capitol group
63 Legal appendage
64 "I never hated a man enough to give him his diamonds back" speaker

DOWN

1 Carry ___ (sing on key)
2 First name of fictional criminal Lupin
3 Big name in hotels
4 Muscle cramp cause
5 "___ and Stacey" (Thomas Haden Church TV series)

6 Dig
7 Desirous look
8 Bring down
9 Commercial suffix with Star and Sun
10 Trade show credentials
11 Homes in the sticks
12 View from Pompeii
13 Lewis : Levitch :: Martin : ___
14 Temerity
21 Gateway Arch architect Saarinen
23 Bright-eyed
26 Female hare
27 Authoritative reference

28 Pauley Pavilion sch.
31 Team color of the San Jose Sharks
32 Hooey
33 Herbal tea type
34 Chalybite and limonite, e.g.
35 Spread made with black olives, capers, and anchovies
37 Every inning has three
40 Chard, for example
42 1954 Humphrey Bogart film
44 Star pitchers?
46 Naval habitat
47 John P. Marquand creation
49 Pole vault unit?
51 Four-bagger
53 Skinny pump designation
54 Leap with a twist
55 Slow seasons at Albertville
56 Soprano Ponselle
60 Clothespin, to a Brit

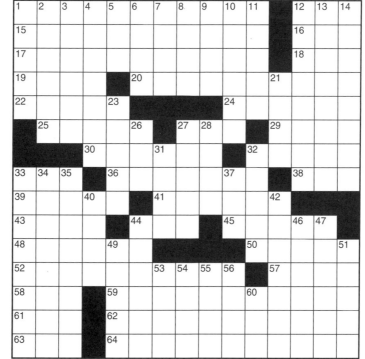

ANSWER, PAGE 79

17

THREE FROM THE BIG TEN

BY DAVID J. KAHN

ACROSS

1 Son of Gordius
6 Hydrous magnesium silicate
10 Arc on a musical score
14 Garnish
15 Procter & Gamble brand
16 Alleviate
17 Celebrity chef DiSpirito
18 Plant of the primrose family
20 Student-parent at Indiana University?
22 Circuits
25 Cover for a cueball
26 Silver medalist behind Yamaguchi at the Albertville Olympics
27 Drift
28 Sound booster
31 Join up
33 Mare hair
34 Attack
36 Work unit
37 Student heroism at the University of Wisconsin?
41 Once called

42 "Can't Help Lovin' Dat Man" composer
43 It can be lunar or solar
45 Brutes
48 Short salesman?
49 Pole
50 Org. that publishes many schedules
51 Liège province town
53 Game similar to euchre
55 Good-for-nothing student at the University of Minnesota?
59 Fighters
60 Varsity

64 "The Electric Kool-Aid ___ Test"
65 Mental faculties
66 Subway
67 Leonardo's costar in "The Aviator"
68 Plum stage role for Plummer
69 Brooklyn's ___ Institute

DOWN

1 Tarnish
2 Lisa Loeb hit from the album "Firecracker"
3 One of Skitch's successors as bandleader on "The Tonight Show"

4 Man of principles
5 Condescending one
6 Spinners
7 Ovid's others
8 Popular Debussy work
9 Independent republic since 1960
10 Infirmary fluids
11 Floats on a seaplane, e.g.
12 Not fazed by
13 Have confidence in
19 More anxious
21 Language related to Winnebago
22 Offshoot

23 Ancient kingdom in what is now Jordan
24 It's filled with scoops
29 TV character who debuted on "Happy Days"
30 Piston rival
32 Brains
35 Raced
38 Make preparations
39 Open, in a way
40 NBA All-Star Game team
44 Map abbr.
45 "Super Size Me" order
46 Vienna debut of 1805
47 Unchecked development of real estate around a city
52 Musical featuring the song "It's the Hard-Knock Life"
54 Tourney winner
56 Secrete
57 "___ baby!"
58 SALT signer
61 LAX guess
62 Exhibit stuff
63 Wisecrack

ANSWER, PAGE 80

THEMELESS 6

BY VICTOR FLEMING

ACROSS
1 Certain Prot.
6 Chicago Seven member
15 Figure skater Cohen
16 Like some headphones
17 In heaps
18 Confront
19 Coined phrase?
21 Temp. unit
22 Range that the Buffalo River flows through
25 A bit, colloquially
29 Become sour
32 Hayes who voices Chef on "South Park"
34 Alaska, once: Abbr.
35 Reply to "Look at that!"
37 Relies on
39 Prolific layer of eggs

41 File
42 Conductor's coworker
44 Sunglasses
45 Stationery store buy
46 Harsh Athenian lawgiver
48 Annual Hanoi holidays
49 Simmers
51 More expensive
53 ___ Tafari (Haile Selassie)
55 Bill Keller is its ed.
59 He tied Grant Hill for the 1995 NBA Rookie of the Year
64 Showing shock
65 Indistinguishable

66 III
67 Element #25
68 Peel's partner in "The Avengers"

DOWN
1 Orr teammate, familiarly
2 Grief
3 Part of an archipelago
4 1933 Mae West film
5 City in Andalusia
6 They're stunning
7 Hudson Bay prov.
8 Underground letters
9 Posterior
10 Vicuñas' habitat

11 "Exactly!"
12 Downturn
13 Repair shop fig.
14 Liberal leader?
20 Restaurant VIP
23 Karen Kijewski's fictional private eye ___ Colorado
24 Rue of "Less Than Perfect"
26 Live
27 Stand on a table
28 Dillon portrayer
29 They work with grout
30 On-line news distribution system
31 Contents of some Jamaican jams?

33 Superficial
36 Particle in a chamber
38 Duke, for example: Abbr.
40 Uncool character
43 "Sweet Hearts" novelist Melanie ___ Thon
47 Wicked thing
50 Present day hero?
52 Les ___-Unis
54 Hide
56 Mule's mom
57 Tool for a duel
58 High-ranking player
59 Nance or Nantz
60 Org. for drillmasters?
61 One with a six-yr. term
62 Winter coat?
63 Article in Der Spiegel

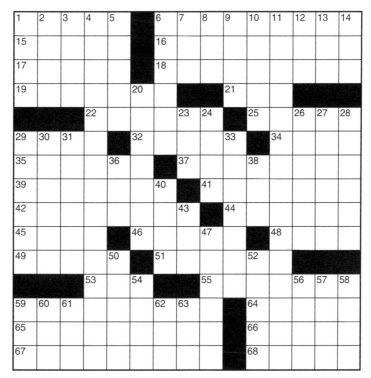

ANSWER, PAGE 82

BABY BOOMERS

BY ANTHONY J. SALVIA

ACROSS

1 Passes on the track
5 "Roger ___"
9 Author of "My Life So Far"
14 Mark's successor
15 Ingrain
16 Step
17 Typical Al Watan reader
18 Drive, for example
19 Beginnings
20 Mortgage figure
21 Cat, in Cataluña
22 Far from friendly
23 Troposphere phenomenon
25 Result of some financial transactions
29 Dir. from Manhattan to Montauk
30 "... ___ flag was still there"
31 Aretha Franklin's Grammy-nominated sister
32 "Nothing runs like a ___" (slogan for a farm equipment company)
35 Impertinent
37 Missouri senator Bond
38 It might be bookmarked
39 Like some furniture
42 "Romeo Must Die" star
43 Apéritif made with white wine
44 Painter Tanguy
45 Member of the L.A. Rams' "Fearsome Foursome"
47 It's impacted by global warming: Abbr.
49 Live

50 ___ hangers (high motorcycle handlebars)
51 Not requiring bleeping
53 Museum piece
57 Golf alternative
58 South Pacific libation
60 Grandpa Walton portrayer
61 Nitwits
63 They travel in style
64 So
65 Dentist's advice
66 The Old Sod
67 Persian Gulf capital
68 Scout master?
69 Stoolies
70 Hawk

DOWN

1 Perk for a corporate executive, maybe
2 Atmospheres
3 Kansas county or its seat
4 Less loaded
5 Genre of the album "Natty Dread"
6 First-string players
7 Hurdle for a would-be doc
8 Seed drill inventor for whom a band is named
9 Military training center in N.J.
10 Prophesying site

11 Lou Holtz once coached them
12 "Deception Point" author Brown
13 Spots on television
24 Them, with "the"
26 Diva's showcase
27 Beam
28 Lace accompanier
30 Beneficial
32 Fists, slangily
33 Hill of CNN
34 Elementary student at Little Dipper School
36 Certain plane
40 Zero's shape
41 1996 A.L. Rookie of the Year
46 Bookkeeping books
48 Up-to-the-minute
50 Drops off
52 ___ profundo
53 In plain sight
54 Cliffside dwelling
55 Stately
56 Waiter under the bridge?
59 Kazakh's home
61 At the rear
62 Pavement warning

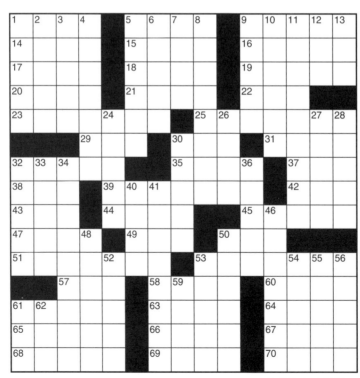

ANSWER, PAGE 84

THEMELESS 7

BY FRANCIS HEANEY

ACROSS
1 Impecunious
16 Rolling Stones album featuring the song "Where the Boys Go"
17 Fume
18 Sol.
19 Unsung worker
20 Dustin's "Kramer vs. Kramer" role
21 ___ particle (electrically neutral meson)
22 It takes up space
23 Order of business
25 Immaculate
29 Dimension alternative
33 Okefenokee Swamp resident
34 Spoken placeholders
35 Soothe
36 Grape-shaped
37 Raquel's "Myra Breckinridge" costar
38 Extremely, in slang
39 Chow chaser?

40 Dry
41 Huff of the Devil Rays
42 Grand ___ (county in northwestern Vermont)
43 Side views on blueprints
45 Feature in an open-air zoo
47 Voice
48 Kind of theater
51 Flight sergeant in the RAF, e.g.
52 Winner's cry
53 Org. with a staff of Aesculapius as its logo
56 Mr. Stohler's job in "Breaking Away"

60 Where the Wild play hockey
61 Argument-ending words

DOWN
1 Saturn's creator
2 1947 Dennis O'Keefe film
3 Goes bad
4 Airline that filed for bankruptcy in Oct. 2004
5 Fish mentioned in "I Am the Walrus"
6 Mallet holder
7 National Puzzlers' League publication, with "The"
8 Karate skill level

9 It may be resistant to inflation
10 Louisiana's most populous parish
11 Interprets
12 OK setting
13 Long
14 Plum pudding ingredient
15 Goddess of childbirth
22 She went undercover as a Playboy bunny
24 Storage unit
25 Activist Klein
26 Pole positions are held by them
27 Bubbly
28 Serenity

30 Author with the pen name Saki
31 Last name in "The Courtship of Miles Standish"
32 Gets old
37 "Careless Hands" singer
38 Christian on the Bounty, e.g.
40 Harbor seal
41 Kanga's creator
44 Seitan worshipers?
46 Without an awkward pause
48 Turn red, perhaps
49 OT book
50 ___ Jeans
53 Whitney of Pratt & Whitney
54 Slugger Williams
55 Collections of miscellanea
57 Paw
58 "There is no ___ except stupidity": Wilde
59 One way the wind blows: Abbr.

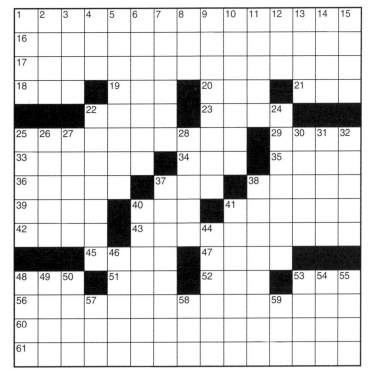

ANSWER, PAGE 86

FASHION STATEMENT

BY ED EARLY

ACROSS

1 Triangular sail
4 Gp. headquartered in Vienna, Austria
8 Turn
13 Nickelodeon cartoon girl
14 Ancient alphabetic character
15 Absurd
16 Start of a quote by Coco Chanel
18 Arctic chunks
19 Best Actress of 1972
20 Kitchen gadget
21 "Serpico" author
22 Lilting syllable
24 Chip's partner
25 Quote, part 2
29 See 32-Across
30 Write over
31 Balabushka product
32 With 29-Across, Robbie Robertson's group
34 Balin of "The Black Orchid"
35 Antiquated

38 Lake in California
40 Cybershopper's site
41 Quote, part 3
46 Actress Campbell
47 ___ favor (please, in Spanish)
48 Dairy stick
49 Puffs up
51 Color similar to turquoise
55 Spotted
56 End of the quote
57 German city that was once part of Prussia
58 "___ quam videri" (North Carolina's motto)

59 Birdsong of the '80s Nets
60 Odd job
61 Pumped up?
62 In need of a change

DOWN

1 "How Important Can It Be?" singer James
2 Mesabi Range feature
3 Seven Sisters college
4 Threatening words
5 "Knit one, ___ two"
6 Authorize
7 Corporate kahuna, for short

8 Mock
9 Centrum rival
10 Round number?
11 Baseball writer Roger of The New Yorker
12 Singer with the album "I Ain't Movin'"
13 Vague
17 Honey substitute?
20 Ingredient in quiche Lorraine
23 CORE piece
25 ___ World Service (international news provider)
26 ___ minérale

27 Magical word
28 MPG-determining group
32 Digital watch abbr.
33 Metal fasteners
35 Antiquated
36 Room for a science class
37 Easter purchase
38 Metal refinery
39 Sully
40 Target of tweezers
41 How some articles are written
42 Of the recent past
43 Despite that
44 Devoured, with "down"
45 On the sheltered side
50 "___ Star" (Kris Kristofferson movie)
52 In that case
53 Module
54 Vulcans, e.g.
56 ___ Peres (St. Louis suburb)

ANSWER, PAGE 88

22

THEMELESS 8

BY ED EARLY

ACROSS
1 Not irr.
4 Credit cards
11 Pop psychology authority?
14 ___ de coeur
15 Robbins's role in "Bull Durham"
16 ___ Khamenei (supreme leader of Iran)
17 Burkina Faso's capital
19 Prohibit
20 Expostulatory
21 Amsterdam, e.g.: Abbr.
22 With 47-Down, third baseman of the 1960s Yankees
23 Author of "Work in Progress"
25 Cereal alternatives
30 Flies like an eagle
31 Uniform
32 Russian provinces
34 "___ Bingle" (Crosby nickname)
35 Splits
36 Montezuma's title: Abbr.
39 Part of a tea set
40 Downsizer
41 College head, in slang
44 Is assured of success
46 Little vixen, e.g.
48 Common footnote abbr.
49 Sitter's bane
50 "I Want to Be Happy" musical
55 Kazoo's center
56 Big books
57 Goof
58 Bush or Texas follower
59 He hit 18 more home runs than Gehrig
60 Twaddle
61 They're often run by children
62 Super ___ (GameCube predecessor)

DOWN
1 ___-earth policy
2 1989 Annabella Sciorra film
3 Longest possible chord
4 Woodworking power tool
5 Chaps
6 Boatloads
7 Turn bad
8 Loose garment
9 "Genius ___ percent inspiration ...": Edison
10 Paratroopers, e.g.
11 Sometime in the future
12 Twist in a criminal plot
13 Bar stock
18 Aged
24 "I'll send an ___ to the world" (repeated lyric in "Message in a Bottle")
26 "Unforgettable" singer
27 Sorcery practiced in the West Indies
28 Camel's cousin
29 Barry and Thomas
33 Bandar ___ Begawan (capital of Brunei)
35 Admit defeat
36 Unjust demand
37 Brood
38 Advance trials
39 XXXVIII × V
40 Heightened, with "up"
41 Celebrex maker
42 Cesar who played the Joker on "Batman"
43 Whiz
45 Skin cosmetics
47 See 22-Across
51 Ga. neighbor
52 Actress Sosnovska
53 Mad Libs request
54 Monkeyed

ANSWER, PAGE 90

CROSS-REFERENCING

BY ROBERT H. WOLFE

ACROSS
1 Blanquette, e.g.
5 Routine
8 Extinct northerner
14 A pop
15 "The ___ Inside" (Best Foreign Film of 2004)
16 Steep-sided valley
17 Race created in 1895
18 Roseanne Roseannadanna's show, for short
19 "Zip it" code
20 Puts on the block
23 Excite
24 "ER" extras
25 Get hooked
28 Word with union and card
31 More, in Madrid
32 Invited
33 Fred who had a famous sneeze in early motion picture history
34 D-s particle, for example
36 Matter
37 City on the Golfe de la Gonâve
40 Sudsers
41 Reagan's second Attorney General

42 Dr. Seuss, to his friends
43 He was enshrined in the Tennis Hall of Fame the same year as Guillermo
44 Stone
45 Like some fourth-quarter kicks
47 Clear
48 College football coach Parseghian
49 Org. concerned with lab safety
50 Popular video game of the late 1990s
55 Clamping down on

58 Vote for
59 Good News! alternative
60 French meat-and-veggie dish
61 Horse with no horsepower
62 Spot for some schools
63 Hard to get
64 High priest of Israel
65 "What You Need" band

DOWN
1 Views
2 Bit of folklore
3 Branch of biol.
4 Although, to a Brit

5 One casting aspersions
6 Horse-man of myth
7 It's 1 on the Mohs scale of hardness
8 Jetties that prevent shoreline erosion
9 Aquino's successor as Philippine president
10 Like only one prime
11 Flat's lack
12 Ride
13 Large parrot of New Zealand
21 What philatelists collect

22 Daze
25 Elk
26 Cut, perhaps
27 Rule
28 Visits unexpectedly
29 Quixote portrayer in 1972
30 Magellan, for one
31 Painter buried in Giverny
32 Another name for Nile green
35 Ape
36 From that place
38 It's similar to chocolate
39 Inside passages
44 Bohemian city
46 Take a trip to the gnu world?
48 Brand of fiber
49 Appropriate inappropriately
50 Donation
51 Small force
52 Remove the slack from
53 Big dino
54 Lubbers
55 Executive washroom users: Abbr.
56 Letters from debtors
57 Ballplayer nicknamed "Le Grand Orange"

ANSWER, PAGE 92

THEMELESS 9

BY DAVID J. KAHN

ACROSS
1 Have no dispute with
8 1987 Wimbledon champ
15 "I had no idea!"
16 Italian Renaissance poet who wrote "Orlando Furioso"
17 House seats are determined by this
19 Letters on letters
20 Construction bar
21 Marble used as a shooter
22 Area commanded by DDE
23 Something great, in older slang
27 ___-standard (ordinary, to Brits)
28 Flooring piece
29 WWII battleground, briefly
30 Word with fours and hours
32 ___ Mae
34 Photographer Goldin
35 Somber notices
37 With 58-Down, 6th-century B.C. Chinese philosopher

38 Tactics
40 Nephew of Abraham
41 Some housewarming gifts
44 Apr. addressee
45 Flight deck abbr.
46 Geologic divisions
47 Child's dosage, maybe: Abbr.
49 Open-and-shut case?
52 Sure alternative
55 Soissons seasoning
56 "It's the end of ___"
57 Tram contents

58 1937 Edward G. Robinson movie
62 Capital of Andalusia
63 Broke in a canine?
64 They get the lead out
65 Tribulations

DOWN
1 "'Twasn't nuthin'"
2 1814 treaty site
3 Big name in kitchen gadgets
4 Repair by adding material
5 Physicist Fermi
6 They usually come with strings attached

7 Youngster who's up all night
8 Jeff Hawkins invention
9 "Here We ___" (Gloria Estefan hit)
10 Unconscious quirk
11 Baked, in Bologna
12 Turkey wing?
13 Some fare-beaters
14 Cupcake
18 Kresge Art Museum locale
24 "My toughest fight was with my first wife" speaker
25 Wrangler, for example

26 Charles's "heir and a spare," e.g.
27 It's often served with mayo
30 Abraham Lincoln, notably
31 "The Loco-Motion" singer
33 Best Actor nominee for "The Fixer"
35 Brother of Snoopy
36 On ___ (how some things are built)
39 Collagen target
42 Mauna ___
43 Less flexible
48 Not impromptu
50 Branford and Wynton's father
51 "Groovy!"
52 Predecessor of de Klerk
53 Whirling
54 Users of slide rules, stereotypically
58 See 37-Across
59 Pub crawl beverage
60 Camera type: Abbr.
61 Mont-___-Anne (Can. ski resort)

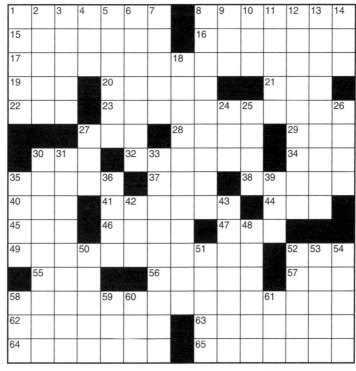

ANSWER, PAGE 94

25

SÍ FOOD

BY GARY STEINMEHL

ACROSS

1 "¡___ mañana!"
6 Dance site
10 Drink made with beaten eggs
14 Communion table
15 Buckeye State county
16 Home of the ABA's Rockers
17 USN officer
18 Inadequate
20 1942 Spencer Tracy movie
22 Chateau ___ Michelle (Washington winery)
23 Vast amount
24 "Forget it!"
28 They're sexy
33 Terre in the Seine
34 Lady's man
35 Texas hoopster
36 Cocaine, in slang
37 Nancy Fairbanks mystery that includes recipes
41 Essence
42 Abbr. in a return address?
43 Gut reaction?
44 "America's Next Top Model" network

45 Celia Cruz sang to it
49 MTV offering
51 They rotate 2,000 times per hour
52 Pointed extremity
54 Head honcho
59 It's never been thought of before
62 ___ Tages (someday, in German)
63 Xenon's lack
64 Halting walk, informally
65 Paris's ___-Cœur
66 Part of HTML
67 "Quit it!"
68 Head lock

DOWN

1 Cease-fires
2 Star in the handle of the Big Dipper
3 It comes at you from two directions
4 Like a tug-of-war rope
5 What crafty people have
6 Mass confusion
7 A in geometry
8 Jazz line
9 Shipmate of Buzz
10 ___ Bandito (old advertising mascot)

11 Mississippi county whose seat is Tupelo
12 "Holiday ___"
13 Word with liquor or sticker
19 Lets go
21 Idyllic locale
25 Ad come-on for a big-ticket item
26 Asphodel's cousin
27 Tree that's a symbol of death
29 Tens' place
30 Rack up
31 "Hotel du ___" (Booker Prize winner by Anita Brookner)
32 Revlon model Mendes

36 Disapproving shouts
37 Language of the Southwest
38 Model Carangi who was played by Angelina Jolie in a TV movie
39 WWW address
40 Least assertive
41 Porsche Cayenne, e.g.
45 Disgrace
46 Creator of Shmoos
47 Letters at Indy
48 They can be sweet or hard
50 He has a powerful thumb
53 Stopping places when heading toward home
55 Memory measures, for short
56 Film cut
57 Movie character with more than 400 siblings, all of whom are killed within the first five minutes of the film
58 Ananias
59 "Hardly!"
60 Bardic work
61 ___ populi

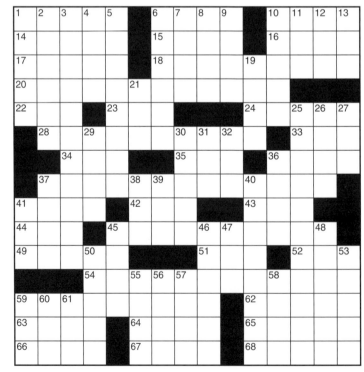

ANSWER, PAGE 96

THEMELESS 10

BY BRENDAN EMMETT QUIGLEY

ACROSS

1 Place next to Pennsylvania Railroad
8 Banded stones
14 Only man to twice win the U.S. Open without losing a set in the entire tournament
15 Excuse
16 Fun times
17 City where the musical genre crunk originated
18 Fifth you can take?: Abbr.
19 Stripper
21 Numbers discussion, maybe: Abbr.
22 Shot
25 They cause havoc, e.g.
27 '40s computer
28 Soli ___ gloria
29 Pay out, with "down"
30 He lost out to Jamie Foxx for Best Actor of 2004
33 "___-daisy!"
34 City near Cologne
35 Cornish speaker
37 Absquatulate
40 Its motto is "Look sharp, live smart"
45 Ingredients in fuzzy navels?
47 Neighbor of Isr., once
48 Big name in china
49 Preventing progress
51 It could go either way
52 It makes leasing pleasing
53 Home to King Fahd Stadium
55 FDR program
56 Women in Journalism postage stamp honoree
58 Looking less healthy
61 Region in Ecuador east of the Andes
62 Locale in Arthurian legend
63 Images on Chinese gold coins
64 Song alternative

DOWN

1 Shot from the air
2 Sports Illustrated's 1971 Sportsman of the Year
3 Decathlete's equipment
4 1860s White House nickname
5 Football Hall of Famer Blount
6 Made a flub
7 Site of underworld bribes
8 ___ Fufkin (Paul Shaffer's "This Is Spiñal Tap" role)
9 Easy-to-swallow tablet
10 "... one leg ___ time"
11 Show nerves
12 Nonresident physicians
13 Role for Glaser and Stiller
15 Black-and-white
20 Got behind
23 Character who delivers the line "To-morrow, and to-morrow, and to-morrow"
24 Imitate
26 Butterfingers
28 "Verbosity leads to unclear, inarticulate things" speaker
31 He outlived his twin brother by a few hours
32 Record of brain activity: Abbr.
36 Composer Schifrin
37 Kind of can
38 Ancient writing system from Crete
39 Join, redundantly
41 Rudolph of "Saturday Night Live"
42 Impart gradually
43 Recently created
44 From one side only
46 "The Handmaid's Tale" character ___ Joy
50 Languishes
51 "Around ___ parts ..."
54 Key of Pachelbel's famous canon: Abbr.
57 It's a good idea to sleep on it
59 Call letters?
60 High shot

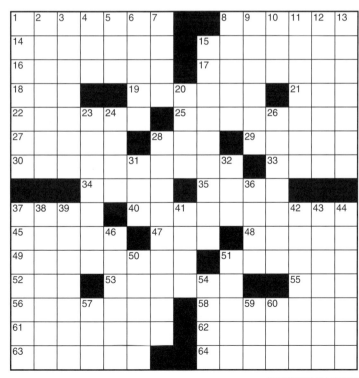

ANSWER, PAGE 79

27

HIDDEN SEASONAL SIGNS

BY TIMOTHY POWELL

ACROSS
1 Telegram period
5 Stigmatize
10 Computer company founder Michael
14 When repeated, a Samoan garment
15 Take in again
16 The first one was made at what is now Chelsea Market
17 Little, a lot of the time
18 For the birds?
19 Color
20 Dizzy spells
23 Undertaking
24 Area 51 sighting
25 Obscure
28 Deli request
34 Mushroom cloud former
35 One doing a farm chore
36 Mean
37 Miffed
38 O.J. Simpson was in it
40 Prepare a pizza
41 Creator of Threepio
42 Predispose
43 "___ in Love" (D.H. Lawrence novel)
44 They go under some athletes' tops
47 Stars at the matinée
48 Missile's path
49 NBC show of the 1960s
51 Clan patriarch, e.g.
58 Soprano Sutherland
59 Extort from
60 Shirking working
61 Emit slowly
62 Down the hatch
63 Wood dresser
64 Ran off the end of the page
65 Night nuisance
66 He was on deck when Bobby Thomson hit "The Shot Heard 'Round the World"

DOWN
1 Pomeranian, for example
2 Cassette contents
3 During
4 With 58-Down, source of a student's income, perhaps
5 Crows
6 Take back
7 Pangaea section
8 How whiskey might be served
9 Washington's were famous
10 Amazon, e.g.
11 Composer Satie
12 Microscope piece
13 Offering at an auction
21 Metrical foot
22 Not too close
25 ___ reader (elementary school book)
26 Heavy wood
27 Like some Greek architecture
29 Nelson Mandela's mother tongue
30 Wee one
31 Car rental chain
32 Hayseed
33 ___ Corning (insulation maker)
38 Chest protectors
39 Shell mover
40 Wrestling maneuver
42 Dig
43 Baby bottom cleaner
45 Wasn't fair?
46 "Annie Hall" character Alvy ___
50 Restaurant row?
51 Implement
52 Level to the ground
53 Partner of savings
54 Beetle, for one
55 "There you have it!"
56 Osbourne of Black Sabbath
57 Bread types
58 See 4-Down

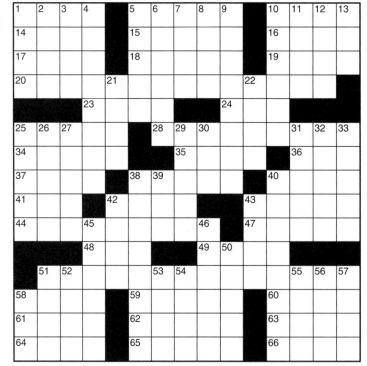

ANSWER, PAGE 80

THEMELESS 11

BY BYRON WALDEN

ACROSS

1 Solo accompanier
10 Color similar to appleblossom
15 Shrimp cocktail?
16 Unrivaled
17 Yawner's self-diagnosis
18 Latin word on some diplomas
19 Cheesecake ingredient?
20 Increase, with "up"
22 When "Dianetics" was first published
23 Got wound up
26 Szmanda of "CSI"
28 Yoshihito's yes
29 Part of many URLs
30 Outside consultants?
33 Band that simultaneously released the albums "Greatest Hits" and "Greatest Misses"
34 Hand-raiser's shout
35 Flu type
37 Diffuse, in a way
38 Lets go of
39 Color of Monet
40 Sonnet whose fourth line begins "A mighty woman with a torch," with "The"
42 Stats for RBs
45 Java, e.g.
46 Caramel-filled candy
47 It's often over a foot
49 Bungles
51 Fraidy-cat
53 Informal greeting
54 Altair, for one
56 1993 Iggy Pop song
59 Cardio option
60 Home to La Nouvelle-Orléans
61 Play with your fingers
62 Tangled

DOWN

1 Sangre de ___ (range in the Rockies)
2 Schnozzola
3 Considering
4 Small songbirds
5 A hottie has a hot one
6 Turkish commander
7 Periods used with ordinal nos.
8 Ready for shipping
9 They're often cast in soap operas
10 Hockey great Neely
11 Jack of "Hot Lead and Cold Feet"
12 Pig's ears, perhaps
13 "That Girl" girl
14 Romantic's counterpart
21 Selects
24 ___ of Aquitaine (Henry II's queen)
25 Political cartoonist who created Colonel Blimp
27 Far from surefire, informally
31 Like some gases
32 Lousy
33 "The House That ___ Built" (spooky kids' book)
35 Views with disdain
36 One who impedes
38 Defeats, as an incumbent
41 "What's your rush?"
42 ___ Council ("Survivor" gathering)
43 The get-go
44 Incapable of littering
48 "___ Eyes Were Watching God" (Zora Neale Hurston novel)
50 "Jungle Book" actor
52 Vice in a French restaurant?
55 Warsaw Pact country: Abbr.
57 Bombay Sapphire, for one
58 Bible book after S. of Sol.

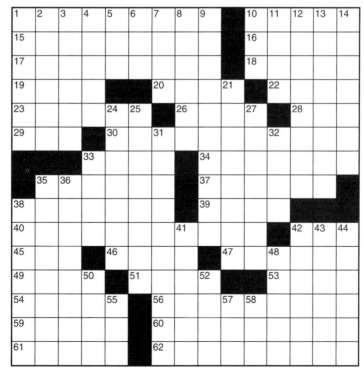

ANSWER, PAGE 82

BODY LANGUAGE

BY PAULA GAMACHE AND VICTOR FLEMING

ACROSS

1 Muscle cars reintroduced in 2004
5 More than just feuding
10 Industry big shot
14 Strawberry soda brand
15 What you might take on a trip
16 Really get to
17 Word with rock and salt
18 ___ Novo (Benin's capital)
19 School that Shelley attended
20 Start of a quip by Groucho Marx
23 Sheepish utterance
24 "Bye!"
25 Queen in a Shelley poem
28 Attends without an invitation
31 Sunblock abbr.
34 What a rough cut might cause
36 Driver's number
37 Bumpkin
39 Middle of the quip
43 Hematologist's study

44 Four-stringed instrument, for short
45 Hightail it
46 Keister
47 Extra
51 Meng-___ (Chinese sage)
52 Organization whose members are at least halfway toward becoming centenarians
53 Sci-fi figures
55 End of the quip
62 Ahi, e.g.
63 Mario's video game brother
64 Mutt on the comics page
65 Fragment

66 Swagger
67 1970 hit by the Kinks
68 Etta of old comics
69 Part of the SAT
70 Exasperates

DOWN

1 Munch like a mouse
2 Boston ___ (MIT, once)
3 River of Cairo
4 Phrase on a platter label
5 Act in, as a TV show
6 God with a belt of strength
7 Threadbare

8 Connect
9 Lease cosigner, informally
10 Doctrine
11 Tubes in a bowl
12 Many times
13 Kevin's "Footloose" character
21 Wet/dry ___ (shop accessory)
22 Course that requires no brain strain
25 Keith Olbermann's network
26 Amtrak train with braking problems
27 Pancetta, e.g.

29 Golden Globe winner Lee
30 Clinch
31 "Ask away!"
32 Places for dips
33 Specialty
35 "King Kong" studio
38 P.D. broadcast
40 Conference pin-on
41 Letters before an alias
42 12-stepper's prayer request
48 End of a warning
49 Teakettle parts
50 Letter two before iota
52 Adjust to the environment
54 Grey Goose rival, for short
55 6, before a slash
56 Complex dwelling
57 Cone bearers
58 Fuego fighter
59 Memory trigger, at times
60 Draw out
61 Nay opposers
62 "That wasn't nice!"

ANSWER, PAGE 84

THEMELESS 12

BY ROBERT H. WOLFE

ACROSS

 1 Cot, perhaps
 9 Masked man of film
14 Of classes
16 Radical leader
17 Like some funds
18 Madison and others
19 Passes the bar?
20 Principle
21 Soak, as flax
22 It "delights by affording a shadow of the pleasure which exists in pain," according to Shelley
24 Grape and others
29 Blinking light, maybe
30 Hiver holiday
31 They're in the arms of Morpheus
36 Loved
38 William Ruckelshaus was its first head: Abbr.
39 Mathematician Andrew who proved Fermat's last theorem
40 Obey
43 Winnow
44 Worcestershire ingredient
45 Sweethearts, in slang
47 Luxury make
51 Bit for Omaha
52 Seascape colors
53 Blessings
59 All, in music
60 Ancient land in what is now Syria and Lebanon
61 Abominated
62 Rubbery polymers
63 TV mom of Alex, Mallory, Jennifer, and Andrew
64 Not subdivided, in a way

DOWN

 1 Ribbies, e.g.
 2 Pasty
 3 Rolls bar
 4 Make good cheer?
 5 Extra piece
 6 Stiff hats
 7 Beset by controversy
 8 Vlasic classic
 9 Not many
10 John Bunyan, for one
11 Excalibur holder
12 Rounded out
13 Janet Jackson hit of 1986
15 "___ la guerre"
23 Buff
24 Punkie
25 Ninth star in a constellation
26 Color similar to pea green
27 Bush-whacked regions?
28 Opera extras, for short
32 Game played in swimsuits
33 QEII part
34 Bank offering, informally
35 They no longer make booms
37 Lounging area
41 New York city that's home to Playland amusement park
42 Get a piece of
46 Right away
47 Clean
48 Peer
49 Like a fruitcake, in more ways than one
50 Kissers
54 Face, in slang
55 Fiddle's family
56 Comedogenic cosmetics aggravate it
57 What polygraphs detect
58 Be cheeky with

ANSWER, PAGE 86

MAKING FACES

BY GARY STEINMEHL

ACROSS

1 Actor Hartnett
5 Gets gangrenous
9 Alley-oop, e.g.
13 Plan for action
14 Statue's place, perhaps
15 Cousin of PDQ
16 Namby-pamby cry
17 Milo of Franco Zeffirelli's "Romeo and Juliet"
18 Like some broadcasts
19 Harmless growth
22 Start of a congratulatory cry
23 Horse operas
24 1971 Best Picture nominee
29 Labor leader George
30 Foe of Carthage
31 Doobie contents
34 Uma's "Be Cool" role
35 One who sniggles
36 Tom's ex before Nicole
37 Halves of quarters

38 Store drawers
39 Term terminator
40 RSVP
41 Two-fifths of MV
42 Neighbor of Portuguese West Africa, on old maps
43 Thoroughly beat somebody up
46 Even though
49 Retina cells
50 Left-handed
54 Addresses that are often underlined: Abbr.
55 Mercedes of "The Fisher King"

56 Number with no complex part
60 Ronzoni topper, perhaps
61 Primavera month
62 Relaxed
63 What the abscissa and ordinate are measured from
64 GPS part
65 Coach K's school

DOWN

1 Super Bowl XV MVP Plunkett
2 Greek chorus part
3 Do some basting
4 Octave twelfths

5 Increase in salary, to a Brit
6 Huit, across the Pyrenees
7 1945 Judy Garland film
8 They spice things up
9 Epicure's pride
10 Bracketed word in a script
11 Relish
12 Exudes
14 Columnist Robert
20 Macy Gray hit from the album "On How Life Is"
21 Harridan
22 Looks for

24 Amorphous organism
25 Began a shift
26 Maker of Golden Twirls
27 Arrive leisurely
28 2001 film directed by Jean-Pierre Jeunet
31 Dust sprinklers
32 Ballplayers Moreno and Vizquel
33 It gets punched a lot
35 Sundries
36 Rambled
42 They hire vets
43 Decennial count
44 Departed in a hurry, with "out"
45 Root canal tool
46 Legend maker
47 Truffula Trees spokescreature of kiddie lit
48 Swell
51 July's birthstone
52 Richard Price novel
53 Teensy amount
57 Évian water
58 Petition
59 NaOH

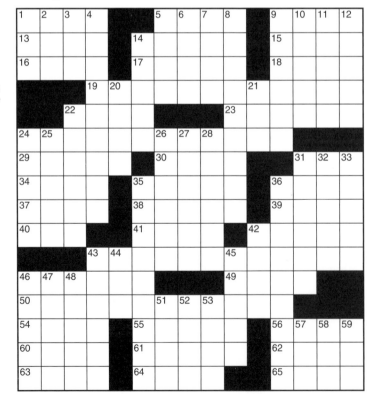

ANSWER, PAGE 88

THEMELESS 13

BY ROBERT H. WOLFE

ACROSS
1 Black garnets
10 Add spice to
15 Ethanol vis-à-vis gasoline
16 ___ Lodge
17 Drop cloth?
18 Lies
19 Behave more wisely
20 Reggae music's Count ___
21 Best Play the year "The Lion King" won Best Musical
22 Cash, in slang
24 Jimmy Dorsey hit of 1957
28 Coca-Cola businessman Candler
29 Frugivorous race of literature
30 Obtuse
37 Exhibits
39 Supporter of women
40 Guts
41 American, to a British monarch
44 Unseen hazard
45 Abbr. on a law firm's stationery

46 Out
48 Olympic gold medalists Jim and Ian
52 Where the Blues Brothers got their start, briefly
53 Ricardo's TV costar
54 1959 Glenn Ford film
60 Six-Day War chief of staff
61 Virtuous one, often
62 They detail heroic deeds
63 Like some questions
64 Competitor of Bobbi
65 Abuses

DOWN
1 Objects of hand wringings?
2 Final, for example
3 Constellation between Cygnus and Hercules
4 Microbiologist's material
5 Delicious drink
6 Essentially belongs
7 Jeer
8 Antepenultimate and penultimate words of the penultimate sentence of a Shakespeare character

9 Penetrates gradually
10 Adjusts the aim of
11 Blade runners?
12 1975 film directed by and starring Kirk Douglas
13 Before
14 Sits still, perhaps
23 Sound of hesitation
24 Like seams
25 Bar with no alcohol
26 Bay and gray
27 Flights, e.g.
31 Initials in the "Hair" song "Initials"

32 Setting of Crater L.
33 WWII acronym
34 Word with house or farm
35 Fifty-fifty
36 Nimble
38 Film genre
42 Hwy. that connects to the Grand Central Parkway
43 It doesn't go in circles
47 One who points a finger
48 Hard-to-make hoops shot
49 Lots
50 Ball carrier?
51 Longtime colleague of Orrin
52 Tennis player with nine Grand Slam wins
55 Language related to Comanche
56 Partition
57 Snorri Sturluson saga
58 V8 vegetable
59 Silhouette, e.g.

ANSWER, PAGE 90

33

BASEBALL FOR THE BIRDS

BY RANDOLPH ROSS

ACROSS

1 Try to influence
6 "___ for Sale" (kids' book by Esphyr Slobodkina)
10 Historic beginning
13 Legend, e.g.
14 Comedian featured in "The Aristocrats"
15 Stop signal
16 Umpire's call that's for the birds?
18 Piece of work?
19 What a cat burglar is unlikely to break into
20 Level of baseball that's for the birds?
22 Pentagonal plate
24 Ford Field players
25 Contemporary of Etta
28 Put the kibosh on
31 Attacked
32 Turn-of-the-century gold rush city
33 Petting zoo sound
36 Swing hard, like a batter's who's for the birds?
40 Pale potable
41 Spun fiber
42 Supernatural
43 Black key next to G

45 Language of Qatar
46 Horoscope columnist Sydney
49 B battery filler?
50 Giants outfielder who was for the birds?
54 Semifinalists in the National Merit Scholarship Program are determined by this
58 Watchdog warning
59 Manager's assistant who's for the birds?
61 At a future time

62 Country records?
63 Reynolds of the Yankees
64 Org. whose logo is an eagle perched on a key
65 Alway's antonym
66 Requiring a lot of attention

DOWN

1 Junior miss
2 Four-fifths of diez
3 Make, as a CD
4 ___ Beach (Brooklyn neighborhood)
5 Schmooze
6 "Let It Snow" lyricist Sammy

7 Tourist destination in India
8 Orange covering
9 Brosnan role before Bond
10 Polite Italian word
11 Already-been-seen TV
12 Barely beats
14 Eye sore
17 Pip ___ (during the afternoon, to a Brit)
21 Give a donation to
23 Response to bad news
25 Nick and Nora are his humans

26 Sway
27 To be, along the Loire
28 Words on a diet food label
29 Big screen name
30 Algebra unknowns
32 Disney feline
33 Rickles remark
34 Et ___
35 Pianist Templeton
37 It has two conferences: Abbr.
38 Costar of Nicollette, Eva, Marcia, and Felicity
39 Person who would not be a good sumo wrestler
43 Wall St. wheeler-dealer
44 Kitchen cooker
45 NAACP part
46 Dr. who delivers
47 Sociological study
48 Trunk line
49 Ruckuses
51 Snack
52 Lecher's look
53 Imminent
55 Mall tease?
56 Base's counterpart
57 Place to swim or take classes
60 Has what it takes

ANSWER, PAGE 92

THEMELESS 14

BY JOE DIPIETRO

ACROSS
1 Letter getters
8 Passport maintenance, e.g.
15 Withered
16 Score of 73, often
17 Wage earner's concern
18 It's NW of Fayetteville
19 Stated in detail
21 Iron man
24 Suffix with percent
25 Enter one's username and password
29 At a later date
30 Not as bright
32 "Good one!"
33 ABC News reporter Potter
34 Storyteller
36 Bug
37 Wages
38 "Are we on?"
39 One who might bring someone in DOA

40 Certain stock trader, for short
41 Turned, in a way
42 Hall of Fame quarterback Luckman
43 Obedience school command
45 Engine malfunction
46 Kunis of "That '70s Show"
47 Unseated
49 Pluralizing Spanish letter
50 Full of crud
51 Snipe, e.g.
54 Guinness competitor
57 Out
61 Newsy dot-com

62 Call for sushi, possibly
63 It grows downward
64 Belt loop attachment

DOWN
1 Seattle summer hrs.
2 Presidential period, perhaps
3 Kill
4 Being
5 Convert to a screenplay
6 Theorbo's cousin
7 Lobby
8 It's not meant for the shelf
9 Protester
10 Protester

11 Enclose, with "off"
12 Lori Loughlin's character on TV's "Summerland"
13 Std.
14 A little bit of work
20 Uncomfortable
21 Blew by
22 In the world
23 Soap lookalike
26 Submits
27 Frozen dessert
28 Like some deliveries
30 Cali coins
31 The ___ Beagle ("Three's Company" bar)
34 Semi
35 Stick

44 Response to one in command
46 Horse that performs well in the slop
48 Slip'n Slide maker
50 "Sanford and Son" spinoff
52 Spread out on the counter, maybe
53 As to
54 Sandwich that would be incongruous to eat on matzo during Passover
55 It's one step from the bigs
56 Racetrack logo
58 Team that plays its home games at the BOB
59 Squash court telltale
60 Name of a famous well-connected man

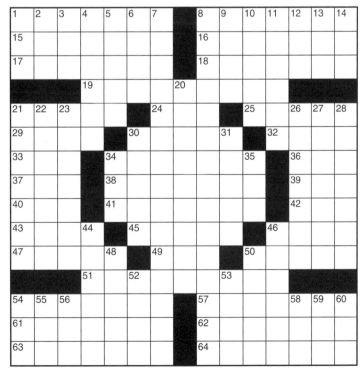

ANSWER, PAGE 94

QUARTERLY BRIEFS

BY LYNN LEMPEL

ACROSS

1 Crimean War figures
6 ___ California Sur
10 Alternative to org
13 In a muddle
14 Leaves wide-eyed
15 City near Brigham Young University
17 Hedonistic way of life
19 Gran
20 Item in an alley
21 Disassembled
22 Cast party?
23 Prepare for broadcast
25 Middy's assent
26 People who put you to the test?
27 Repudiation
29 Tour phase
30 Grandstand cheer
31 Grasps
32 Gary Sinise TV series
34 Unassertive
35 Deficiency (and an alternate title for this puzzle)
38 Unusually qualified
41 Ratify
42 American League division
45 Saldaña of "Guess Who"
46 Swab
47 In the existing circumstances
49 Football flub
51 Where QB Chris Weinke won the Heisman
53 Baseball's all-time leader in slugging average
54 Went astray
55 Moves like a moth
57 Clifton of the 1950s Knicks
58 Roll of stamps
59 Smelly toilet water
61 Cooking fat
62 Caulfield of "Buffy the Vampire Slayer"
63 Greenland native
64 Rugby touchdown
65 Sly look
66 Word with statute or suit

DOWN

1 Chosen
2 Progress
3 Utterly foolish
4 Architect Koolhaas
5 1986 #1 hit for Starship
6 It doesn't include overtime
7 Sentient
8 "Bad Reputation" singer
9 Burier of Pompeii
10 Dream up
11 Figures of speech?
12 Shammes's place
16 Like a bog
18 Find from Down Under
22 Colorful socks
24 Associations
26 Elizabeth of "La Bamba"
28 Hangdog
29 Morale booster
32 Prune
33 NASCAR supplier
36 Durian feature
37 Hyena's hangout
38 Tenochtitlán ancients
39 Express with no restraint
40 Scottie, e.g.
43 It's a shocker
44 Shakespeare's queen of the fairies
47 Shutter speed setting
48 "Fiddler on the Roof" setting
50 Uniqueness
51 Water park slide
52 Motorcycle add-on
55 Movie set at New York's High School of Performing Arts
56 Lose ground
59 Gulper ___ (deep-sea fish)
60 "Blastoff" precursor

ANSWER, PAGE 96

THEMELESS 15

BY BRENDAN EMMETT QUIGLEY

ACROSS

1 "Happy Days" catchphrase
8 Kawasaki products
15 Letter getter
16 Unusual objects
17 Boston suburb where N.C. Wyeth was born
18 Pierces with many holes
19 Bargain basement abbr.
20 1961 Ermanno Olmi movie
22 Cry from the safety inspector of Springfield Nuclear Power Plant
23 Max of "The Prizefighter and the Lady"
25 Da and ja
26 High-level programming language
27 And what follows: Abbr.
29 Feline
30 "Vision of Love" singer
31 Immediately precede
33 They have no chance
34 Subject for the sculptor Phidias

35 Paris parish priest
36 Try to make a date with
39 Agent's goal
43 "Best Week Ever" channel
44 Occupational suffix
45 Olympic swimmer de Varona
46 Mainz article
47 ___ Commission (corruption investigation at which Frank Serpico testified)
49 Division politique
50 D.C. baseballer, for short

51 U.S.-launched orbiter that photographs the earth's surface
53 Doctor from the planet Gallifrey
54 Draw on
56 Joins together
58 Mukluk wearers
59 Pertaining to flight technology
60 Subway alternative
61 Brand of shaving cream

DOWN

1 Florida's ___ Island
2 Repeat
3 Russell of Hollywood

4 Former
5 Black cherry soda maker
6 1982 World Cup winner
7 Uproars
8 A.C. setting
9 Leaves
10 Flap
11 Not automatic: Abbr.
12 County of Ireland
13 Freeze up
14 Moves sideways
21 Capital south of Lillehammer
24 Either end of a gridiron
26 Unknown defendant
28 Line (up)

30 Prepared, as apples
32 Lay
33 Luger, e.g.
35 First-aid giver
36 "I'm Not Wearing Underwear Today" show
37 Popular massage technique
38 Book subtitled "Across the Pacific by Raft"
39 Out of play
40 Fold
41 Where the Los Angeles Angels play
42 1887 Victorien Sardou play on which an opera is based
44 Hudson River school painter George
47 Simple membranophone
48 Distance runner Nurmi nicknamed "The Flying Finn"
51 Describe
52 Fruity Pebbles rival
55 "He's Just Not That Into You" coauthor Tuccillo
57 Frasier's producer on "Frasier"

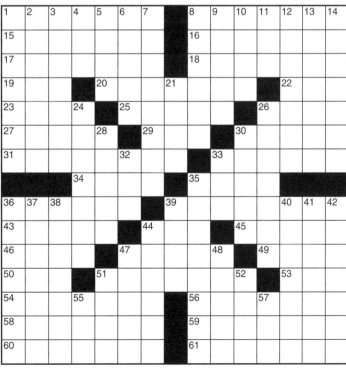

ANSWER, PAGE 79

HAMMING IT UP

BY JOSH STRAYHORN

ACROSS

1 "Bejabbers!"
5 Makes a selection
9 Huckleberry, e.g.
14 Young salmon
15 ___ Loma (Toronto landmark)
16 Cursor mover
17 Keiko, for one
18 Citation abbr.
19 Periodical
20 Check out the inside of a Ford?
23 Long
24 Singer with the album "Starpeace"
25 Give a thumbs-up to
29 Smoker's conversation piece?
32 World leader?
33 Metal whose purity is measured in quilates
34 '80s Norwegian pop group
35 Fussy old woman
38 19th-century globetrotter

39 Desired gift in "A Christmas Story"
41 Loonie's denomination
42 Setting of L. Okeechobee
43 Not saying a word
44 Situation at the start of a concert by singer Nicks?
50 City near Los Angeles
51 Published
52 By means of
54 Mexico and Spain?
57 Crush
60 Razor sharpener
61 How doodles are drawn

62 Dostoyevsky novel, with "The"
63 Signs one's name to
64 Pseudoarchaic adjective
65 Office e-mails, maybe
66 Former
67 Part of ABS

DOWN

1 Strong adhesive
2 Loft
3 Mysterious knowledge
4 Heavy cart
5 Home of the fictional character Winston Smith

6 Regular
7 Bygone big shot
8 Mouth-watering?
9 Polished
10 Delaware State player
11 Slow bear's fate, perhaps
12 John Cougar Mellencamp's "R.O.C.K. in the ___"
13 He won an Oscar for playing Mohandas
21 Cornball
22 Ho-hum
26 Grenade that shatters, for short
27 Bishop Museum locale

28 "Sleepless in Seattle" costar
30 It might be taken before a trip
31 ___ Heights (Six-Day War battleground)
35 Company whose slogan is "Better sound through research"
36 Like JFK, say
37 Adjudge
38 Leading
39 Very well-done
40 Rolls-Royce's parent company
42 Bash
43 Most malicious
45 Extremely implausible
46 Entrances
47 They're often boiled
48 With gusto
49 Gives up
53 Still
55 Role for Moira in "Chaplin"
56 El Paraguay y el Uruguay, por ejemplo
57 "That's the guy!"
58 Olympionic, e.g.
59 Net holder

ANSWER, PAGE 80

THEMELESS 16

BY ROBERT H. WOLFE

ACROSS

1 Old warships
10 Adherence
15 1994 John Waters movie
16 "Hill Street Blues" actress Veronica
17 Play ender
18 Agape, perhaps
19 Produced by land deterioration
20 Leaves in a bind?
21 Indication of recognition
22 They check for poison
24 Energetic person
28 When round one of a PGA Tour event is typically played
29 Suit tail?
30 Grecian Formula rival
37 Give another piece to?
39 Most wanted list abbr.

40 It might have a face value of a thousand bucks
41 Order request at a greasy spoon
44 Times
45 End of a professor's e-mail address
46 Fiona, e.g.
48 Eighth notes
52 That guy, to Guy
53 Last name of brothers in the International Motorsports Hall of Fame
54 Make sibilant, perhaps
60 Dino's love
61 The Furies

62 Blabbermouth
63 Like the scrub jay
64 Makeup of some buns?
65 The Golden Flashes of college sports

DOWN

1 "Cast Away" setting
2 Keister
3 About
4 Minor shortcomings
5 Taj Mahal, e.g.
6 His debut album was "Radio"
7 Rectify
8 ___ Ana (Las Cruces's county)

9 Refine
10 Pitch-and-run
11 "Diane" actress
12 Picture
13 Less experienced
14 Emmy winner Sharon
23 Org. involved in the Branch Davidian raid in Waco
24 Whittle
25 Horny goat
26 Part of a ladder back
27 Color also called Italian green
31 Mideast alliance inits., 1958–61
32 Enjoy Killington

33 Former South Korean president Roh ___ Woo
34 R.J. Reynolds tobacco brand
35 H lookalikes
36 Cape
38 Actualized
42 Abyssinian covering
43 Most unpleasant
47 "The ___ win the pennant!" (repeated shout from Russ Hodges, 10/3/51)
48 Docks
49 Like some goals
50 Unified
51 Bit
52 Light measure
55 Come-on
56 Light air
57 Flash in the brainpan?
58 Hearty enjoyment
59 Cato's being

ANSWER, PAGE 82

FIRST-RATE

BY JAY LEATHERMAN

ACROSS

1 Band with the album "Afterburner"
4 Jalopy
8 About 624 billion electron-volts
11 Unwinding sound
12 Fuddy-duddy
14 ___ chi ch'uan
15 Paramyxovirus component
16 Chevy model
17 POTUS's alternate title
19 State
21 Annoyance
23 Big Apple airport abbr.
24 Tabloid twosome
26 Litterbug, for example
28 Abstract
30 Actress in "Samson and Delilah"
31 Lush
33 Org. that has many probes
35 ___ means
36 Now, in Novara
37 A-1 condition
40 Split the deck
41 Sarah Clarke's "24" role
43 Comedic routine
44 "Dick Tracy" villain
46 Total
48 Plead to get
50 What an underline might indicate
52 Small remnant
53 French department in the Midi-Pyrénées region
54 Say Kaddish, e.g.
56 "Be that as it may ..."
60 Hide in the shadows
62 "Cyrano de Bergerac" playwright Rostand
64 Inflation-fighting org. during WWII
65 Game prop
66 Island near Bora Bora
67 State dinner wear
68 Half of a breath mint
69 Former Soviet news agency
70 Buzzed

DOWN

1 Holder for a handleless coffee cup
2 Novelist Grey
3 Loser to "Mutiny on the Bounty" for Best Picture
4 Class after phys ed, perhaps
5 If you had it, you wouldn't need this clue
6 Without delay, for short
7 Stacks
8 Catchall abbr.
9 Train part
10 Thin cookie sweetened with treacle
12 Smoker's mouthpiece
13 What a bell signifies at a track meet
18 Comedian in AT&T ads
20 Spare change?
22 Skipper's syllable
25 Capital on a tributary of the Berezina
27 Diplomatic hdqrs.
28 Observe Arbor Day
29 Honorific in India
31 House bigwig of the '70s and '80s
32 Hard copies
34 Filled to excess
38 Very hush-hush
39 Honorific in Turkey
42 Catch a bug, say
45 Lethargic
47 Dead letters?
49 Some government funding
51 Time's 1977 Man of the Year
55 Jewish youth org.
57 Info that might make a bettor better
58 Magnum ___ (great work)
59 Readily molded
61 Dumped doll
63 Sue Grafton's "___ for Outlaw"

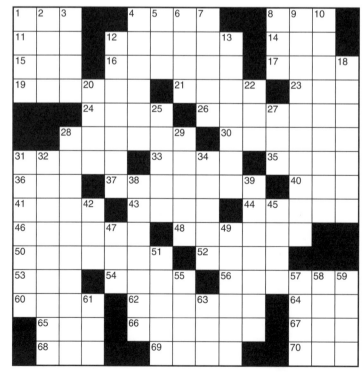

ANSWER, PAGE 84

40

THEMELESS 17

BY RAYMOND HAMEL

ACROSS

1 Chill
6 Ninnies
11 Mag revenue source
14 It has its ups and downs
16 K's lower it
17 Have smooth sailing
18 Shaving goo
19 Tapped-out person's letters
20 Kick out
21 Worry about, in slang
23 Proof goof
25 Religious doctrine
27 She retired with 158 international goals
28 Cherished
30 Central African Republic border river
32 Endangered species with a long snout
35 Roman goddess of the hearth
37 Scientific calculator button
38 #1 hit of 1972
41 First word on many spines
42 "Water Music" composer
43 Fuses, perhaps
44 Crystal clear things?
46 Pulitzer-winning biography of 1935
48 Nicollette's "Desperate Housewives" character
49 Tender-hearted person
51 Partner of circumstance
55 Formal acts
57 Try to get home safely, perhaps
59 It often has an upper crust
60 Penn State rival
61 Revival meeting shout
64 Israeli city near Ben-Gurion Airport
65 Complain loudly
66 Navigation dir.
67 Makes an effort to locate
68 Cabezas, across the Pyrenees

DOWN

1 "Credit or ___?"
2 First name of Football Hall of Famer Crazylegs Hirsch
3 Prepare for driving
4 First family member
5 Flatten
6 Flip for
7 Conical lab container with a narrow neck
8 Instituteur's institution
9 "Just Shoot Me!" actress Laura ___ Giacomo
10 Centimeter-gram-second units
11 Lesbians are surrounded by this
12 Song on R. Kelly's "Chocolate Factory" album
13 Places of drudgery
15 Sends a written message to by cell phone
22 "Huh?"
24 Passing notice
26 Dress-up box garment, maybe
29 "___ Ben Jonson!"
31 Wash up
32 Hamlet, e.g.
33 Vincent Price's costar in "The Fly"
34 Abundance
36 Not very often
39 Speedskater who won three gold medals in Lillehammer
40 "David Copperfield" villain
45 Witness
47 Tattooed lady of song
50 "Purlie" co-librettist Davis
52 Footnote abbr.
53 Tigger's creator
54 Looks through a crack
56 Important men
58 Formerly, formerly
62 ___-Bo
63 Got fed up?

ANSWER, PAGE 86

ALTERNATE SPELLING

BY PATRICK BLINDAUER

ACROSS

1 HSBC Arena player
6 S&L offerings
9 Common musical symbol
14 Near
15 Berman who writes for The Nation
16 Say "y'all," say
17 One who's not up at noon
19 Minimal
20 ___-friendly (green)
21 Cookout crashers
22 Aces
23 Inconsistent communication (or what can be found at 39-Across)
26 Sitcom costar of Betty and Estelle
27 Like the numbers dos, cuatro, seis, ocho, etc.
28 Legislator's creation
31 Mitigate
34 Exmaple, for example, for example
37 Domed domicile
39 See 23- and 50-Across

42 Prefix with grain and lane
43 Memo abbr.
44 Raison d'___ (for the good of the country)
45 Didn't observe Yom Kippur
46 There are 100 in a cwt.
48 Bodybuilder's six-pack
50 Ring result (or what can be found at 39-Across)
57 Aware of
59 They're high and mighty
60 Clarke of "Frankenstein"
61 China's Zhou ___

62 Aces
64 Item on the cover of Pink Floyd's "Dark Side of the Moon"
65 "___ My Sons" (Arthur Miller play)
66 Went berserk
67 Site of brave deeds, perhaps
68 RFK's constituency, once
69 Bodings

DOWN

1 Seat of Marion County in both Illinois and Oregon
2 Primitive calculators
3 It's not a cheap shot
4 Sitcom costar of Betty and Estelle
5 On-line brokerage firm
6 Kshatriyas, e.g.
7 Gussy (up)
8 Peppermint Patty, to Marcie
9 "Calm down!"
10 Ham spice
11 Thinks highly of
12 Adam's apple spot
13 Marshes
18 Cell body?
22 Goat quote
24 Rival of Maltin
25 Pitcher feature

29 Setting of a 1978 hit song, with "the"
30 Grounds for a suit
31 1996 movie based on an 1816 novel
32 Be up against
33 Receipt
35 It's used to make beer
36 Dab
38 Shot in the dark
40 Twiddle one's thumbs
41 Special talents
47 Playbill paragraph
49 Café
51 "___ porridge in the pot nine days old"
52 Decoration under a dish
53 They're married to countesses
54 Mental picture
55 Like a Quaker breakfast, perhaps
56 They must be met
57 "Jesus ___": John 11:35 (shortest verse in the Bible)
58 Dictator's phrase
62 Attic spinner
63 Wild butter

ANSWER, PAGE 88

THEMELESS 18

BY DAVID J. KAHN

ACROSS

1 Allen and others
7 Like go
15 Figure in Dante's "Inferno"
16 First Lady whose maiden name was Duarte
17 Mother of Paris and Hector
18 Fireball
19 God of both wisdom and war
20 More unnatural
22 Moving part in a machine
23 Spleen
24 Gladdened, with "up"
25 "Proud ___" (hit of 1969)
26 Berger of "The Glory Guys"
28 Track lines: Abbr.
29 Helping
30 Fawned on
32 Listener
33 Tony-winning role for Nathan Lane
37 Yodeling spot
38 Is overcome
40 You can see right through it
42 ___ Darya (Asian river)
43 Have another go at
44 Lashes
45 Orange areas
47 Dreidel, e.g.
48 Modern address ending
49 Not as skewed
50 "Titanic" heroine
51 Baker's base
53 Spanish royalty
55 Hewlett-Packard headquarters
56 Heavyweight offensive
57 Heavy weight
58 Advance again

DOWN

1 Use of imitative words
2 Nickname of basketball's Olajuwon
3 Ecuadoran estate
4 Make ___ for it
5 Head, slangily
6 Muddle
7 Tony-winning role for Gregory Hines
8 Rara ___
9 Like a lot
10 Copycat
11 Mint
12 Violinist Morini and namesakes
13 1957 Jimmy Dorsey hit
14 Opposition
21 Locale of a semilunar valve
24 Gewgaw
25 Atrabilious
27 Odessa residents
29 Post office machines
31 Humdinger
32 Count ending?
34 "Now ___ done it!"
35 Become fond of
36 "Ran" director
39 Uses, as onionskin
40 Outcast
41 Muhammad's trainer
42 Noble Brit
44 Sports card company
45 Willie of the '80s Chicago Bears
46 Overthrow, maybe
49 Rushee recruiter
50 Cambodian cash
52 ___ anglais (English horn)
54 The way the wind blows, perhaps

ANSWER, PAGE 90

RR XING

BY VAN VANDIVER

ACROSS

1 Ted alternative
8 Actress Plato
12 Crossword writer's activity
13 Most Iraqis, e.g.
16 Snuff stuff
17 Serengeti youngsters
18 Greenish parrot of New Zealand
19 Razed
20 Skiff movers
23 Change of a movie scene?
25 Name-dropper, perhaps
26 In style, old-style
27 Nonpro?
28 ___ d'Ivoire
29 Segal and Fromm
31 Cornfield sound
34 Cantatrice's offering
35 Like the Essex House hotel in Manhattan
36 Hog the spotlight
38 Drug company dept.
40 Cross letters
42 Gals. and qts.
43 Make tracks, maybe

44 Film producer Zukor
46 Stork relative
47 "Story ___" (erotic novel by Pauline Réage)
48 Vamp's scarf
49 Detective created by Rex
50 Painful punch result?
53 Harry who played the Artful Dodger in Roman Polanski's "Oliver Twist"
54 Government health insurance program
55 Envoy letters

57 C-worthy
58 Fine dinnerware
62 Dwelt
63 Shrimp ___ (Japanese restaurant offering)
64 Some PC screens
65 Cold war weapon?

DOWN

1 RR Xing
2 "Evil Woman" rock band
3 Spa spot
4 Ornament for a fowl's nose piercing?

5 Dog bane
6 Like some checks
7 ___-defense (psychological mechanism)
8 It's served before beddy-bye
9 Consumed, Bible-style
10 Food packaging abbr.
11 Soc.
13 Token opening
14 Star of "Taxi"
15 Tube with charged atoms?
19 Auction nod du jour?
20 Washington has two

21 Polar explorer's wear
22 Corkscrew-shaped pasta
24 Regarding this point
30 Newspaper clipping
31 Did a thorough search of
32 Togs
33 Big oil company
37 Augusta police?
39 Buggy bounder?
41 More unkempt
45 Pharmacy notation
47 Brother of Set
50 Word with scarlet or yellow
51 Latin phrase that's often abbreviated
52 Drawn
54 Children's book author Brown who created the "Arthur" series
56 First year of the 31st century
58 U.K. business name ender
59 Visceral
60 Time
61 ___ Ysidro

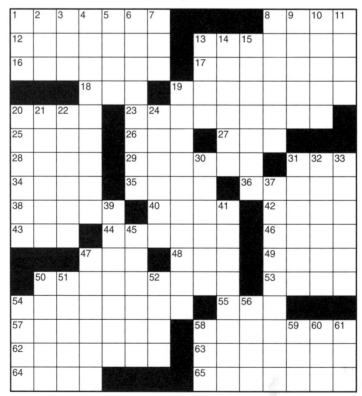

ANSWER, PAGE 92

THEMELESS 19

BY Victor Fleming and Bruce Venzke

ACROSS
1 Roone Arledge was once in charge of it
10 Triathlete's problem
15 Gets loaded
16 It may have crude content
17 Risky whiskey
18 Accord
19 Like pins and needles
21 Like "Charlotte's Web"
25 Some roof jobs
29 Fox relative
31 Family members?
32 Ride attire
33 Item on a tub ledge, maybe
36 Actor ___ Avery
37 Future, e.g.
38 Roquefort source
39 Euphonium's fundamental pitch
41 Neighbor of Man. and Minn.
42 Waggish
44 Dior cut
45 Jeremy's friend in the comic strip "Zits"
47 A.C. Green was one
49 Disgruntled person
52 Ale alternatives
53 "Sentimental Journey" bandleader
55 It's paler than amethyst
58 Trousseau container
63 David whose products suck
64 Non-tandem bike
65 Lines used in Cartesian coordinates
66 Stretching sites

DOWN
1 Diebold product
2 Class with a lab
3 VIP with an MBA, perhaps
4 Fig. in identity theft
5 They might be offered to avoid bouncing
6 In heaven
7 Strap on Omar Khayyam
8 Hammer's partner
9 Fishhook line
10 Offsets
11 Welcome, as a new era
12 She played Jennifer in "Love Story"
13 Intersected
14 Be a busybody
20 Globe Theatre baddie
21 They have retractable roofs
22 Hall of fame
23 Bully, at times
24 Denom. affiliated with the University of the South
26 Meshed up?
27 Bit of paronomasia
28 Food preservation experts
30 Twisted treat
34 Sharp punch
35 Former Georgia senator Miller
40 Immobile Stratego piece
43 Golf course designer Jones
46 Tighten, perhaps
48 The Rangers' div.
50 Despise
51 Stingless flier
54 "And Morning ___ with haste her lids" (line from Emerson's "The Problem")
55 It's been cured
56 "Tucker's People" novelist Wolfert
57 Avenue between Park and Third, familiarly
59 Medicine ___, Alberta
60 The Normandy Campaign was part of it: Abbr.
61 Equinox mo.
62 ___-80 (old computer)

ANSWER, PAGE 94

45

SEEING THE SITES

BY JOE DIPIETRO

ACROSS

1 Chooses
7 New York Shakespeare Festival founder Joseph
11 Overcast, e.g.
14 Stumblebum
15 Piece with a cadenza, maybe
16 Volos vowel
17 Lizard of the Southwest
19 Fashion
20 Out of the trap?
21 Tracks
22 Creator of Muff Potter
24 Comics character with a horse named Spark Plug
27 Some session starters
30 Treater's words
31 Beat
32 Color similar to old china
37 Park your carcass
38 Joey's home
39 Personal ad abbr.
40 International cricket competition
43 Anniversary gift after leather
45 Spree
46 NFL team, for short
47 "Young Einstein" filmmaker
52 "Access Hollywood" cohost
53 Bewitched
54 Region on a Risk board
58 Pemmaraju of Fox News
59 South American wide body
62 Puzzle
63 Socks
64 "Access Hollywood" cohost
65 Ottawa-to-Halifax dir.
66 Flew
67 Handles

DOWN

1 Frozen breakfast brand
2 Sanctum
3 Pamplona pronoun
4 Mine holder
5 Actor Arnold
6 UConn's setting
7 Hit hard
8 Affected, in a way
9 It has a shell
10 Start of a series
11 Wasteful thing?
12 PayPal's bailiwick
13 LaPierre of the NRA
18 14th Hebrew letter
23 Uterus
25 "Go on ..."
26 Genre derived from punk
27 Intense craving
28 Anthony's XM radio cohost
29 Loses one's job
32 One who is quite a downer?
33 Robitaille of the Los Angeles Kings
34 Innsbruck interjection
35 One in a needle program
36 A dog's age
38 NFL team, for short
41 Shop item
42 Bread and cabbage
43 Sch. with a Brooklyn campus
44 Fire up
46 "Gimme a sec"
47 Start of an AOL alert
48 They do work on the spot
49 Clear
50 Leveled
51 Microsoft's was in '86
55 No good deed
56 Marsh growth
57 Joe holders
60 Unruly head of hair
61 What a triple with one on gets you: Abbr.

ANSWER, PAGE 96

46

THEMELESS 20

BY JOE DIPIETRO

ACROSS
1 Ghetto ___ (boom boxes)
9 Repeat
15 It leads to the tympanic membrane
16 Quincy, in the comic strip "FoxTrot"
17 Handlebar alternative
18 Suburb of Boston
19 Martin of the Nashville Predators
20 Engine with a combustor
22 Family tree word
23 Hat, in slang
24 Foxy
25 "___-in' in the Wind" (episode of "The Simpsons")

26 Some contracts
28 French composer Charpentier
30 Loosen, as a cap
33 To ___ (just so)
34 Heron variety
37 Southern constellation near Telescopium
38 Memorable dummy
39 Let go, with "off"
40 Sailor
42 Kind of penguin
44 Divides
48 Storm maker
49 Check out
52 Laugh sound
53 They're hard when they're ripped

54 Spanish Harlem grocery
55 Goldie's daughter
56 Bonehead
58 Player with a Super Bowl XVIII ring
60 Like some spicy cuisine
61 Welcome symbol
62 Car bombs?
63 Fell apart

DOWN
1 Happened to
2 Amy's husband in "Little Women"
3 Fleet
4 "Get lost!"

5 You might get one in a booth
6 Cover with a hard coating
7 Auto racing's Bobby
8 Stop hitting?
9 Pesto tidbit
10 Semiprecious stones
11 Rural road feature
12 Plan B time
13 Glance
14 Listen
21 Curve cutter
24 Wail for a while
27 Glove material
29 Urich's role on "Vega$"
31 Fought
32 Heat source?

34 Refinement
35 Turkey, for example
36 Rejoinders
38 "Heartland" autobiographer Mort
40 Hockey team coached by Wayne Gretzky
41 Formula One rival of Ferrari and Renault
43 Charge again
45 Secretly follow
46 Component of some showers
47 1962 #1 hit by the 4 Seasons
50 Under the deck
51 Slack-jawed
55 Radiohead album of 2000
57 Misery
59 Zeus's form when he seduced Eurymedusa

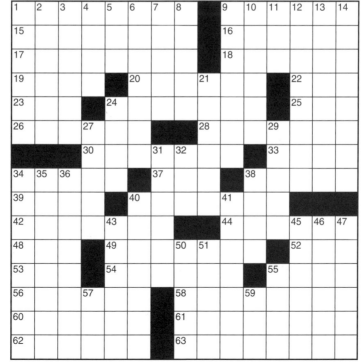

ANSWER, PAGE 81

47

WANNA BET A SILK PAJAMA?

BY JOHN R. MINARCIK AND VICTOR FLEMING

ACROSS

1 Like some centers
7 Pinup's pin
10 Hose hitch
14 Nimoy costar
15 Thick brick separator?
16 State of mental confusion
17 State on the Isthmus of Tehuantepec
18 Popeye's "goil"
19 Model who dropped Abdulmajid from her professional name
20 Put the star of "Ecstasy" in ecstasy?
23 Mr. Universe's pride
26 Gigayear
27 Vessel in a recess
28 "Jeopardy!" rarity
29 Wax nostalgic about a Spanish region?
33 Source of linseed oil
34 Angular distance from the equator: Abbr.
35 Woman with sobrinos
36 Work on the bar, perhaps
38 Concave cooker
40 Frequent costar of Olivia
44 Multinational group headquartered in D.C.
46 Chocolate retriever, for short
48 Sludge
49 Delivery program for dummies?
53 Last word of Kipling's "If"
54 Silver by a plate, maybe
55 Sister of Helios
56 "Excelsior" is its motto: Abbr.
57 What Ogden Nash bet didn't exist (despite 20-, 29-, and 49-Across)
61 Is mendacious
62 WC
63 Eastern floor mat
67 Itinerary guesstimates, briefly
68 Part of MRE
69 Like shorelines, often
70 Cold capital
71 Factor in a QB's rating
72 Inspire awe

DOWN

1 Bustle
2 Hawaii's Mauna ___
3 Deli delicacy
4 Kewl
5 Griffiths of "Six Feet Under"
6 Being watched over by Lady Luck
7 Canterbury can
8 Refugee's request
9 Youth in a Banana Republic, maybe
10 Level
11 Shea Stadium star of the '60s and '70s
12 Hank who voices Apu and Moe on "The Simpsons"
13 Type
21 One who comes with a tied knot?
22 Sandy's owner
23 Sandy's sounds
24 Alnitak, Alnilam, and Mintaka form a famous one in the night sky
25 Mark for life
30 Postulate
31 Palm site
32 Bounce
37 Pop solidly
39 Superman's real name
41 Stable color
42 Sharon's husband
43 ___ Summit (city in Missouri)
45 Latke-making need
47 Swollen
49 Pitches incredibly well against
50 Fantastic
51 Transfer, as data
52 Capital of Eritrea
53 Pope who negotiated with Attila in 452
58 "Put a tiger in your tank" gas company
59 Much
60 How some lists are arranged
64 Chisel kin
65 Leo succeeded him as manager of the New York Giants
66 Chemical suffix

ANSWER, PAGE 83

48

THEMELESS 21

BY BEN TAUSIG

ACROSS
1 Pitchers Nipper and Leiter
4 French friar
8 Flips over
14 Chitlins and ham hocks, e.g.
16 Sitting Bull's language
17 Investors pay it
19 Den luxury
20 12/13, e.g.
21 Reason to keep playing
22 Folded flier
26 Alice doesn't work here anymore
27 False
30 Withdrawal need
31 Extra minute?
32 Engels subject
36 Crayola color since 1949
37 One of the Ramones
38 CDC's city
40 Henpecked person's acquiescence
41 Baby Bop, to BJ
42 Endgame result, sometimes
44 Start of a common run
46 Say again
47 Quote from Homer
48 Scrutinize, with "over"
49 Slim change
53 Doll up
58 Yellow member of the Teletubbies
59 Thoroughly enjoy oneself
60 Cleveland Indians, perhaps?
61 Virginie, par exemple
62 "Livin' Thing" band

DOWN
1 "Uncle Moses" novelist Sholem
2 Stuff with shells
3 Apt. overseer
4 Sternward
5 Jungle hugger
6 Landlocked country of S.A.
7 More out there
8 Kryptonian, e.g.
9 Dojo levels
10 Endorsements
11 Bad plan
12 Amazon, for example
13 They're blown in the winds
15 Mansion employee
18 Relevant, in law
23 Negative particles
24 Michael Jordan, e.g.
25 Prefix with centenary
26 Artistic blend
27 "___ miracle!"
28 Ingenious
29 Marks down
30 Boom box button
33 "A Passage to India" heroine
34 Candidate's goal
35 Scant
39 Texas player
40 "Star Trek: The Next Generation" character Tasha ___
43 Go through odontiasis
44 Throw
45 Cockroach repellent
46 Scintillas
48 Oct. ordeal for many teens
50 "Natural Affection" playwright
51 It might be in a mess
52 Pump name
54 Radical leftist gp. that had an emblem of a seven-headed cobra
55 Milliner's offering
56 Gabrielle portrayer on "Desperate Housewives"
57 March Madness souvenir

ANSWER, PAGE 85

ONE STEP AT A TIME

BY PETE MULLER

ACROSS

1 Sunset setting
8 Examples of low life?
15 WWII battle site
16 It has and is filling
17 Seismograph record
18 Green Day drummer
19 Everywhere
20 Namely, after "to"
21 Half of a TV sitcom duo
22 Schoolyard game
26 Passport datum
27 They last, on average, 730½ hrs.
30 Pair-___ (two-person racing shell)
31 Day break
33 NYC's original subway line
34 Got to third base, perhaps
35 In need of a shower
39 Like some choral performances
42 Unearthly
43 Lake west of Carson City
44 Color similar to mermaid
46 Not alert
48 Tha ___ Pound (rap duo)
49 Trail mix morsel
50 Telecom giant
51 Modern test subject

52 Bananas
53 One of the folks
56 Winter melon
60 Place apart
62 Country partially within the Arctic Circle: Abbr.
63 Country estate
66 Horseman, at times
68 Saying
71 Hawaiian erupter
72 Mackenzie's "One Day at a Time" costar
73 Ones who prepare fillets
74 Film that was Bette Midler's starring debut

DOWN

1 Angry
2 Creole stew vegetable
3 Iranian coin
4 Well-off
5 Where Ali beat Foreman in "The Rumble in the Jungle"
6 Personal
7 Harpy
8 In "Macbeth," it starts with the line "Thrice the brinded cat hath mew'd"
9 Bushy-tailed relatives of weasels

10 Where the needle is when the gas light is lit
11 Lesotho, to South Africa
12 Unwanted guests
13 Without help
14 Heat-resistant glass
20 Puzzle invented by Lewis Carroll (and a hint to this puzzle's theme)
23 Viagra spokesman
24 Attacks, with "at"
25 Possible source of salmonella poisoning

27 Mazda roadster
28 Ferocious two-tone mammals
29 Safer coworker
32 Look
34 Oration
36 Odeum, for example
37 Bind
38 Broadway role for Bea Arthur
40 Prothalamion, e.g.
41 ___ aunt (British advice columnist)
45 Old-fashioned exclamation
47 Panasonic rival
53 Checkers, e.g.
54 Jelly made with spiced tomato juice
55 Childbirth assistant
57 Radio reporter Raum and romance writer Roberts
58 Tours school
59 "It doesn't matter"
61 Short pass
64 Space opening
65 Author of "Armageddon: A Novel of Berlin"
67 Nice street
68 Future specialist, maybe: Abbr.
69 Part of a cheer
70 Natural buzzer

ANSWER, PAGE 87

THEMELESS 22

BY JOHN FARMER

ACROSS

1 "Goodness gracious!"
7 Long while
14 Lewis's land
15 Swallows, as snake oil
16 Base
17 Moved to the right
18 Soap opera actress Kristen
19 One sporting three stars: Abbr.
20 "___ Es el Amor" (Eydie Gormé album)
21 Minister
22 Subject of Edward Hopper's "Nighthawks"
23 George Orwell's real first name
24 Jolt
26 "If I ___ Love You" (Squeeze song)
27 Dwarfs of folklore
28 1987 N.L. Rookie of the Year Santiago
29 XKE's make, for short
31 Elmo, e.g.
33 "Conjunction Junction" word
34 Like Godot, in "Waiting for Godot"
36 Grifters
38 Pix
39 Listen attentively
42 Collette of "In Her Shoes"
43 Acts as an informer
44 "Red, White & ___" (heavy-metal compilation album)
45 Undesirable name?
46 Belts
47 Skiing gold medalist at Calgary and Albertville
48 Barbarous
50 Signs from above?
51 Monastic garment
52 "Eichmann in Jerusalem" writer Hannah
53 Phoenicians, e.g.
54 Some spreads

DOWN

1 Kind of inspection
2 Newton contemporary
3 Source of "Say! In the dark? Here in the dark! Would you, could you, in the dark?"
4 At great length
5 Fitting figure
6 Rick's pile
7 Thin ice, e.g.
8 Like a big sister
9 Hockey Hall of Famer Sather
10 Tax form ID
11 Check accompanier, perhaps
12 Takes up, as a career
13 Triage expert
15 Hotel amenity
19 Lightweight shirt material
22 Fiend
23 Essen article
25 Quinces, e.g.
26 Kishke casing
28 Deep-sea diver's hazard, with "the"
29 Come thisclose
30 State
32 Fireplace tool
35 It might be left of center
37 Puts into ciphertext
39 Rain forest climbers
40 Morning love poem
41 Undergoes a chemical change
43 Kentucky Derby winner sired by Seattle Slew
46 Net Nanny target
47 Said three times, a 1970 WWII film
49 Longtime employer of Helen Thomas
50 Atomize

ANSWER, PAGE 89

"ACHTUNG, BABY!"

BY JOY M. ANDREWS

ACROSS

1 Word with name or age
7 Like "Fat Albert"
14 Spanair rival
15 1993 Nirvana album
16 Keen
17 Creator of the religion Bokononism
18 Some bots
19 Setting of the Dasht-i-Lut desert
20 Stir
21 Worked over
23 Where travel guidebook writer Karl Baedeker was born
25 "Monsoon Wedding" director Nair
28 Apologue
30 Dig deeply
32 Toddler's untouchable?
33 Last name of a trio of baseball brothers
37 Singer Marvin Lee Aday, familiarly
39 Lanai lass
41 Janet's role in "Psycho"
42 Good places to make a scene
44 MPAA part
45 Prerequisite for diff. eq.
47 Divided
48 Peekaboo player's shout
51 ___ Mujeres, Mexico
52 Make blank
55 Salon jobs
57 Blame
58 T-bone's locale
60 Spine line
64 Assured
66 She played Susan on "Suddenly Susan"
67 Silver eagle wearer
68 Drooped
69 Irregardless
70 College application parts

DOWN

1 Not piquant
2 Bridge support
3 GOPer's rival
4 ¼ Dutzend drinks?
5 Fiorentino of "The Last Seduction"
6 Enjoys to the max
7 Former Los Angeles mayor Richard
8 Actress Chlumsky
9 Miniature golf feature
10 When crême glacée is most popular
11 Manet contemporary
12 Bluenose
13 Boarded
17 ⅓ Dutzend pilots?
22 Rebecca's "Risky Business" role
24 ½ Dutzend guns?
25 "___ Mia!"
26 Suggestion box fillers
27 Nature calls?
29 Place for some flakes
31 "Rockaria!" band
34 Phnom Penh money
35 "___ It Sleeps" (1996 Metallica hit)
36 Elf-produced cracker brand
38 At the moment when
40 When "GMA" airs
43 It can be dragged and dropped
46 They catch a lot of waves
49 One-named Tejano singer
50 Still in decent shape
52 The unmarried woman in "An Unmarried Woman"
53 Talked incessantly
54 With cogency
56 What German shepherds earn?
59 Comply with
61 Adios's counterpart
62 ___-doke
63 Baseball team from Ohio
65 Reporter's question

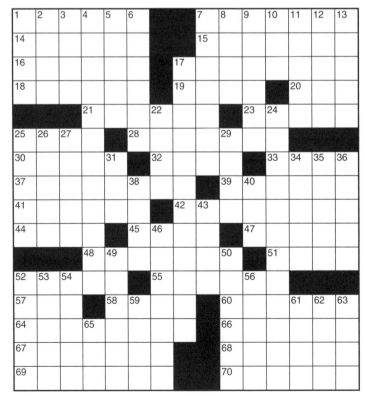

ANSWER, PAGE 91

52

THEMELESS 23

BY BRUCE VENZKE AND VICTOR FLEMING

ACROSS

1 Place for the down-and-out
16 "The evidence suggests ..."
17 1959 Fredric Brown mystery
18 Nathan and Matthew's "Producers" director
19 Anti-___ (airplane devices)
20 Winter cap parts
26 Teacher's sheet
34 It can be shocking
35 Lou's "La Bamba" costar
36 Saint ___ Bay (inlet of the Atlantic)
37 Is raised all the way up and then back down to the midpoint
45 Tabloid headline writers, often
46 "You need to get on with your life!"
47 Ingredient in some salads
51 ___ Janeiro
56 Classic Disney parody
62 Newman's Own product
63 Department store underlings

DOWN

1 Search engine count
2 Koko Head's locale
3 Tussaud and others: Abbr.
4 Elegant elephant of kiddie lit
5 Most economical
6 Ivy League sch. setting, more often than not
7 ___ Mère Église, France
8 Diatonic scale tone
9 Government loan org.
10 Maxi edge
11 "Kyrie ___"
12 Clarence's role on "The Mod Squad"
13 French bean
14 Perpetually
15 Loser to "Chariots of Fire" for Best Picture
21 Is in another form
22 Triple Crown jockey Turcotte
23 Part of UCLA
24 Aramis, to Athos
25 Word with bono or rata
26 Pan handlers
27 "La Marseillaise" composer Claude Joseph Rouget de ___
28 Teletubbies' shout
29 Recoils
30 Hindu title
31 Talking Heads member Weymouth and others
32 Young partner
33 Staff symbols
38 Deli meats
39 Took a course?
40 Shrike ___ (Australian bird)
41 ___ polloi
42 Social worker?
43 Time delay
44 Glad handler
47 Pitchfork-shaped letters
48 "___ way!"
49 Grown-up pup
50 Storybook story
52 Mrs. Victor Laszlo
53 Actor on "thirtysomething"
54 Power
55 Flat ones are extremely bad news
57 Bleat
58 Walk-___ (small parts)
59 Paper revenue source
60 Lingual opening
61 Basketball Hall of Famer Unseld

ANSWER, PAGE 93

WHAT THE ELL?

by Randall J. Hartman

ACROSS

1 Ear's spears?
6 Check no.
10 "What are the ___?"
14 Already
15 Island west of Lombok
16 Get over a hurdle
17 Make rhapsodic
18 See 6-Down
20 Apartment, often
22 Balanced
23 Winter celebration in Vietnam
24 High vantage point
26 "Dingbat" of '70s TV
28 Trial separation?
30 Start of a soliloquy by Hamlet
32 Manipur man's title
35 Charge
36 With 37-Down, 1976 Pulitzer winner
38 First name in smiles
40 Outstanding
42 Manolete's conquest

43 See 32-Down
45 Source of "Woe to them that are at ease in Zion"
47 "That's amazing!"
48 Erich Kästner's title boy
49 Cause to make a mistake
51 Casa brick
53 Argues
57 ___ Rafael, California
59 Improve
61 "The miracles of science" sloganeer
62 With 64-Down, "How to Play With Your Food" authors

65 Diminutive
66 Wall-to-wall measure
67 Major ending
68 Breakfast order
69 Creator of Hi and Lois
70 Off-pitch
71 Entangle

DOWN

1 Cube-jumping arcade game of the 1980s
2 U.S. president who sired 15 children
3 Silly as a goose
4 Role for Radcliffe in several films
5 Pullover, e.g.

6 With 18-Across, 1945 Pulitzer winner
7 Champs Élysées eatery
8 Apple cider spices
9 Tuckered out
10 Over the hill
11 Final shot
12 Big dog breed, familiarly
13 Word with soft and sweet
19 Rita's "West Side Story" role
21 Short-horned grasshopper
25 Noodge
27 Publicize
29 Table finish
31 Logroño's river

32 With 43-Across, thinks something is up
33 Major-league career leader in at bats
34 So to speak
36 Examined, with "out"
37 See 36-Across
39 Vapid
41 In the center of
44 Airline to Hawaii
46 Bedroom communities, often
49 Serve
50 New Guinea native
52 Shipmate of Scotty
54 Nuku'alofa is its capital
55 Register
56 Fashion
57 Zombie computer output
58 Designed to reduce wind resistance
60 Senate shout
63 Larry's father on "Curb Your Enthusiasm"
64 See 62-Across

ANSWER, PAGE 95

THEMELESS 24

BY KAREN M. TRACEY

ACROSS
1 "Boston Legal" Emmy winner
7 Brickbat
14 Crescent-shaped
15 Took a dare
16 Tingling sensations
17 Coming up
18 ESP, e.g.
19 Small rocket on a spacecraft
21 Class with a take-home, open-book, true-false final, say
22 Martin Luther King Jr., e.g.
24 Sarcastic laugh
25 Sweet and soft, in music
26 Merlin Olsen's team
28 "The wolf ___ the door"
29 Cruel treatment
30 Hill of Judas Priest
33 Back door, perhaps
36 Mary ___ cosmetics
37 Blue
38 Put a name to
39 Lampooned
40 Hygienist's advice
41 Unkempt
44 "Piece of cake!"
46 "The Thin Blue Line" director Morris
47 How sun-dried tomatoes might be sold
48 Nav system calculation
49 Spinone ___ (hunting dog)
51 He was Starsky to Soul's Hutch
53 1995 Stephen Rea cable movie about a serial killer
54 Having a money-back guarantee
55 Bad falls
56 Gym wear

DOWN
1 Experience back trouble
2 Sails
3 Subordinate
4 Code word
5 Without beginning or end, archaically
6 Dash button
7 Buck slip attachment
8 Having four sharps
9 Festive decoration
10 Some crystalline compounds
11 Temper
12 "From Russia With Love" actress Lotte
13 Rocker Winter
15 It occurs a little over six weeks after Groundhog Day
20 Like the Taipei 101 skyscraper
23 When Hamlet says "Alas, poor Yorick!"
24 Dispatch
27 Greet eagerly
29 Hockey infraction
30 Krakatoa's country
31 Boosts one's grade, perhaps
32 Comic actor of the 1920s and '30s
34 "Granted ..."
35 Is unwell
39 Unemotional
40 Inactive
41 German empire
42 Adventurous airplane of kiddie lit
43 Persona non ___
45 Communicates silently
47 Getaway spots
50 Gassy prefix
52 "You ___ Love" ("Show Boat" song)

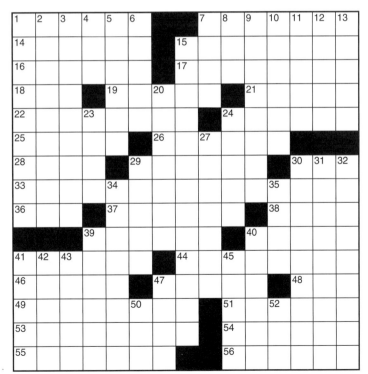

ANSWER, PAGE 81

X OUT

BY LEE GLICKSTEIN AND VICTOR FLEMING

ACROSS

1 Sit for a master
5 40,468,564^{28}/$_{125}$ square centimeters
9 Pronounce
14 Physical love
15 Contest for pacers?
16 Want badly
17 Wraps (up)
18 Cold turkey purveyor
19 Enjoyed
20 Commented on fireworks
22 Like some highways
24 Revolutionary line
26 Word in a bus schedule
27 Nicky of "Boston Public"
30 The tip of the iceberg might be used to make this
32 Bedrocks
34 Chamber sound
35 Lobster spawn
36 Beam
37 Jazz singer Waters
38 Pricker

39 Do a tricky surfing maneuver (and a hint to this puzzle's theme)
42 First word of "Scarborough Fair"
43 Picante
45 Egyptologist's discovery
46 1951 All-Star pitcher Garver
47 Kitchen bar
48 "Scram!"
50 Fiscal exec
51 Make a mistake
52 Gig bag contents
53 Galería display
55 Moves slowly
58 Becomes
61 Birchbark, e.g.

63 Sign of boredom
65 Subject preceder
66 Take home
67 Morales of "Paid in Full"
68 Trading acronym
69 Cared for
70 Low flower
71 "... nobody can ___"

DOWN

1 Tip of Tijuana, perhaps
2 Crispy creme treat
3 Gingrich biographer's inquiry?
4 Chelmsford's county

5 Recipe word
6 Props in "The Hustler"
7 Waxing nostalgic over cheap jewelry?
8 Cure-all
9 Flo-Jo's alma mater
10 Tchotchke
11 Get back into the dating game?
12 "___-Olution" (2002 rap album)
13 Rare color
21 Boat on a boat
23 Warmup sounds for divas
25 Actress Mia of "Ferris Bueller's Day Off"

28 1994 Denis Leary comedy
29 Holy city?
30 Texas county that's Spanish for "arms"
31 First editor of The Atlantic Monthly
33 "Gunga ___"
37 Sportscaster Dick whose memoir is subtitled "Oh My!"
40 When repeated, excessively affected
41 Hermione portrayer in the "Harry Potter" movies
44 Final layer
48 8 pts.
49 Some daisies
54 ACE, e.g.
56 Noble man
57 Pull
59 Suburban warbler
60 Alluring
61 ER measurements
62 Miss. abutter
64 Put an end to

ANSWER, PAGE 83

THEMELESS 25

BY JAY LEATHERMAN

ACROSS
1 The Missouri R. forms part of its border
5 Sch. with five campuses in the Bay State
10 Maker of the Comfort 3 razor
13 Creator of the film characters Harry and Sally
14 Nickname for Alexander
15 Actress Adams of "Junebug"
16 The State Department, informally
18 Cry convulsively
19 De facto
20 Piglet producer
21 Mariposa lily variety
22 Possible response to "Can I, Dad?"
25 He was always very close to his brother
26 Valvoline rival
27 Very hot
28 High end?
30 Busy airport
32 Clotho, Lachesis, and Atropos, with "the"
33 Does well during finals week

37 Diminish
40 Ball attire
41 Teen malady
45 Ladies of Spain
48 The world's best-selling beer, for short
50 Mauna ___ (brand of macadamia nuts)
51 Struggled in water
54 Touched down
55 Narc employer
56 Only Billboard hit for the Spanish group Mocedades
57 "Oysters ___ season"
58 Not flipped, in a way

60 Breadcrumb carrier
61 Bases' counterparts
62 The Missouri R. forms part of its border
63 Spanish ayes
64 Back-to-back French Open winner of the 1980s
65 17th-century actress Nell who was Charles II's mistress

DOWN
1 Summer treat
2 They're worn in pairs

3 Mythological giant with 100 eyes
4 Olympic crafts
5 Spirit of Hope Award org.
6 Taiwanese island off the coast of China
7 Fur family
8 Missourian's demand
9 Dooley Wilson's most famous role
10 Perfect game spoiler
11 Costar of Sid on "Your Show of Shows"
12 Steve Austin and Jaime Sommers, for two

16 Steely Dan cofounder Donald
17 William Jefferson ___ IV (Bill Clinton's name at birth)
21 Rock layers
23 Penguin in "Bloom County"
24 Lummoxes
29 Didn't play
31 Cricket need
34 Huge particle physics lab in Europe
35 Brit's subway
36 Oozes
37 Concerning
38 Chopin contemporary
39 Consecrates
42 At hand
43 Traffic directive
44 Finish off
46 Cite as evidence
47 Ushered to one's seat
49 Fearless
52 Corporation div.
53 Cover with droplets
58 Teammate of Reggie, Rollie, Catfish, and Vida on the 1970s Oakland A's
59 Haute couture initials

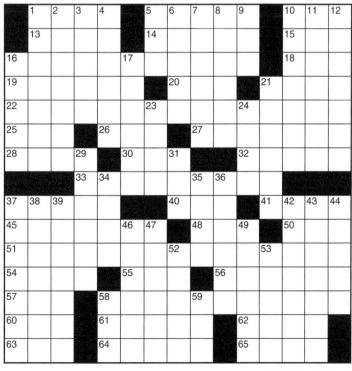

ANSWER, PAGE 85

HOLLYWOOD SQUARES

BY JEFFREY HARRIS

ACROSS

1 Instinctive
4 "Ars gratia artis" studio
7 Emit coherent light
11 Tree with silver-gray bark
12 Like most bachelor's degree programs
14 Bush country?
15 Honey maker
16 High-school military prog.
17 Dwells (on)
18 Fatigues
20 Husband of Pompeia
22 Tarnish
24 What skating on thin ice might get you into?
26 1998 figure skating gold medalist Ilia
27 Richie and Potsie's pal
28 Bird mentioned in "If I Had $1000000"
29 Ritalin treats it: Abbr.
30 Sweating setting
32 Either "New York Minute" costar
34 Like Yanni or Raffi
36 Judge in the Old Testament
37 "Another Green World" musician
38 Big celebration for a high schooler
41 Cut up, as onions
44 Holes at the bottom of a scorecard?
45 Ore. neighbor
48 "A Theory of Semiotics" author
49 Admits
51 "Leda and the Swan" poet
53 Protective glass cases
55 Put in hock
56 Street magician David
57 Had the gumption
58 Brecht's "Threepenny Opera" collaborator
59 Offensive, in a way
61 Diminish, with "up"
64 Finish in the top three
65 Birds on Canadian coins
66 Christian, e.g.
67 Filled a sketchpad
68 Decide (to)
69 Topic of "The Hite Report"

DOWN

1 Shoot the breeze
2 Resulting good
3 Marlon Brando film
4 Resinous substance found in incense
5 Metros and Trackers, e.g.
6 Slab of concrete under a house
7 City on a tributary of the Brahmaputra River
8 Makes bubbly
9 Chief
10 Start of something?
12 Ray Bolger film
13 Soda brand since 1905
14 Bruce Willis film
19 "___ tu" (Verdi aria)
21 Nucleotide used in energy transfer: Abbr.
22 Caribbean music genre
23 Strong joe
24 Toothed tools
25 Part of ERA
27 Plant with yellow flowers
31 Ovid's "I love"
33 Set aflame
35 Once known as
36 Quaint scream
39 Lavs
40 Molly Ringwald film
41 Coming-out party honoree
42 Labatt product
43 Crash
44 Pertaining to the north wind
46 Got some goose down, say
47 '60s psychedelic
50 Delivery vehicle
52 Lea lass?
54 Show with Michael Tucker and his wife Jill Eikenberry as a married couple
55 House coat
57 Go down
58 A-bomb, e.g.
60 Cote noise
62 Bard's preposition
63 Levy

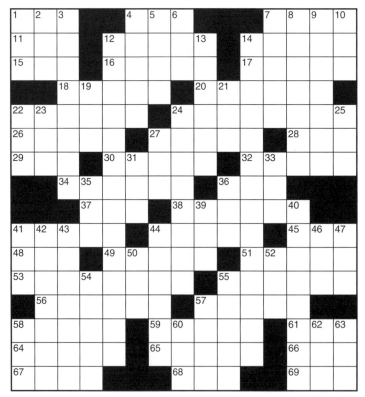

ANSWER, PAGE 87

LIFE GETS IN THE WAY

BY PAULA GAMACHE

ACROSS

1 Virtual PC runners
5 Take the wrong way?
9 PC programs
13 Foil alternatives
15 Paella ingredient
16 Compete in the Kentucky Futurity
17 Small-town skyline feature
18 *When you might meet for a drink*
20 *Super Bowl break*
22 Prickly pear producers
23 Canton that borders Valais
24 Sets in some gyms
25 Alabama, e.g.
27 With a light touch
29 Rear
30 The Pigeon R. forms part of its border
31 Fishtank problem
32 Bookkeeper's stamp

33 Paper section
34 *"I'm not making this up"*
37 Physics topic
40 Place for a dummy
41 There are five in a lustrum
45 Stately street liner
46 Eye piece
47 One-named one-hit wonder who sang "You Gotta Be"
48 Insulin regulates the amount of it in the blood
50 Yacht sail
51 Wharton graduate's deg.
52 Slang

53 *Show on before "Fantasy Island," with "The"*
55 *The latest in fashion*
58 Cream
59 Presque ___, Maine
60 Word with double and check
61 Less usual
62 Slumber party attendee, typically
63 Realise, with "out"
64 Musical character who sings "Leavin' fo' de Promise' Lan'"

DOWN

1 Nuts
2 Dress
3 Fan's place, often
4 Bondman
5 Fat units
6 Widespread
7 Don't just talk
8 Spelldown
9 Fighting
10 Blue book collector
11 Omen
12 Mt. Misery's setting
14 Colonist
19 Some boom boxes
21 Climbing ornamental
25 Rather
26 Edit menu choice

28 Designs on skin, for short
29 They're 15 inches square
32 Pasta name that's Italian for "quills"
33 Mates' assents
35 Malihini serenaders, for short
36 Microbrewery product
37 Blockbuster
38 Court order
39 Ignore local customs?
42 Tall wardrobe
43 Gives back, in a way
44 Ushers, e.g.
46 Loads
47 XLII × XII
49 Rumsfeld's predecessor
50 Outback babies
53 Honorary degrees for attys.
54 Tell all
56 Cable channel with the slogan "Very funny"
57 "10 Things I Hate About ___"

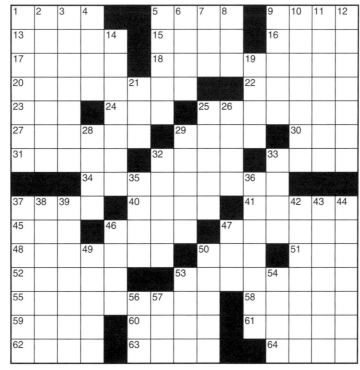

ANSWER, PAGE 89

59

THEMELESS 26

BY OGDEN PORTER

ACROSS

1 Obliquely
7 2003 Billy Bob Thornton movie
15 Key of Schubert's "Unfinished" Symphony
16 Censors, at times
17 Combinatorics topic
19 "Roses ___ red ..."
20 Signal for a fastball
21 Longtime Red Sox announcer Martin whose signature call was "Mercy!"
22 Kin of -kin
23 Part of I-278
27 Impudence
28 Winds up on stage, maybe
31 First song on Genesis's "Genesis" album
34 Meshed setting
36 Faze
37 Actress Meyers
38 Glasses of water, at times
40 Washington Square News is its paper: Abbr.
41 "Out!"
43 Lo-fat
44 Gramps's exclamation
45 Kangaroo Island critter
46 Compete
48 The only player to hit a walk-off home run in a World Series Game 7
54 Cary's "I'm No Angel" costar
56 Grazing locale
57 Letter accompanier: Abbr.
58 Knock-knock joke's punch line, usually
59 "Seriously ..."
63 Guide
64 Jet setter?
65 Don't go out
66 Antithesis of fancy

DOWN

1 Joanna Lumley/Jennifer Saunders series, for short
2 Egotist's look
3 Defame, in a way
4 It starts and ends in inverno in the Northern Hemisphere
5 "That's totally wrong"
6 Still
7 ITV alternative
8 Like some skirts
9 Fix
10 Edamame eater's discards
11 Rainy mo.
12 Singer of "Southern Man" and "Old Man"
13 Olive, e.g.
14 Abbr. on an underling's business card
18 Dominant
24 First name on the album "Voice of the Xtabay"
25 Winner at the inaugural Latin Grammy Awards
26 Pugilists' org.
29 New Age singer from Gweedore, Ireland
30 Breeding stallion
31 Conceal
32 With the bow, in music
33 Women's magazine of the 1990s
35 Frequent poster to an on-line forum, e.g.
38 Compact
39 Even
42 Kristofferson's costar in the TV movie "Freedom Road"
44 Band with keyboardist Richard Tandy
47 Centipede's place
49 Brought on
50 Head of a house of ill repute
51 ___ fence (item erected to annoy a neighbor)
52 Glory
53 Like radon
54 War room fixtures
55 Legions
60 Shift, for one
61 Choler
62 Become interested, with "up"

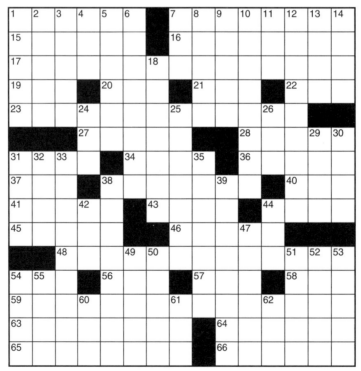

ANSWER, PAGE 91

60

DECISION MAKERS

BY OGDEN PORTER

ACROSS

1 Wilmer Valderrama's role on "That '70s Show"
4 Book whose title character "had lived nearly twenty-one years in the world with very little to distress or vex her" at the start of the story
8 Colgate rival
13 Last hit for the J. Geils Band
14 Night light
15 Camry ___ (Toyota model)
17 Member of 38-Across
19 Upholsterer's fabrics
20 Member of 38-Across
21 Support wires
22 Bossy part
24 Nipped
25 White ___ (hard brownish wood)
28 Rich supply
30 ___ Nova (14th-century music style)
31 Member of 38-Across
35 Hems (in)
38 Theme of this puzzle
43 Sitzmark creator
44 Member of 38-Across
45 Sundance Film Festival setting: Abbr.
48 Tangier, e.g.
50 Actress Brenneman
51 Unemotional person
54 2005 horror sequel with the tagline "Oh yes ... there will be blood"
58 Turnery maker
59 Member of 38-Across
63 Chefs Ducasse and Dutournier
65 Members of 38-Across
66 A score, barely
67 Israel's defense minister before Menachem
68 Snickering sound
69 Concerning
70 Plant also known as dasheen
71 Yossarian's tentmate in "Catch-22"

DOWN

1 Members of the mulberry family
2 Copydesk change
3 Man-to-man alternative
4 Reporter assigned to a military unit
5 Rubber's spot
6 Tidbit
7 Sigourney's director in "The Ice Storm"
8 Left turn from Süd
9 Sit
10 Member of 38-Across
11 Bobby Sherman hit subtitled "If I Had You"
12 Member of 38-Across
16 Gps.
18 "Law & Order" spinoff, familiarly
23 Member of 38-Across
24 Makes hotter, with "up"
25 It might result in a TD
26 "Keep it down!"
27 Weeder's tool
29 Monk's title
32 Slush pile contents: Abbr.
33 Symbol of the American Ornithologists' Union
34 Heat source
36 ___-warrior (environmental activist)
37 Very small amount of money
39 "___ Momo" (1989 David Byrne album)
40 Hagen of "The Country Girl"
41 Sleep acronym
42 Go
45 Lombardy's capital
46 Member of 38-Across
47 Super Bowl XXXIV losers
49 Japanese criminal organization
52 Title for 23-Down
53 Slow, in Italian
55 German river that flows to the North Sea
56 First few bars
57 Reggae singer Kamoze
60 Bounce back, in a way
61 Tick's host, maybe
62 Belgian river that flows to the North Sea
64 Setting of the Druze Mts.
65 Intense black

ANSWER, PAGE 93

61

TWO BITS

BY ANTHONY J. SALVIA

ACROSS
1 Reduce in scope, with "down"
5 Crooked
10 Cannonball, e.g.
14 Mark follower
15 Christopher of "Deathtrap"
16 Italian opera singer Pinza
17 Jejune
18 What waltzes are written in
20 Drive goals, often
22 Zero
23 Look of lust
24 MPG part
25 Stock report info
30 NFC North team
33 Action-oriented person
34 "Groovy!"
35 Defraud, with "off"
36 Divisions of Mexique
38 Boardroom bigwig
39 College in Loudonville, New York
41 Compass pt.?
42 Winter Palace ruler
44 Beatty and Buntline
45 Results of haymakers, perhaps
46 Where sub orders come from
50 Eighty-six
51 Beech family members
52 Web site
55 Addition
60 Gridiron play
62 E-mail recipient, e.g.
63 Swearing-in ceremony highlight
64 Go blading
65 Beer buy
66 Complimentary
67 Wrote a letter, maybe
68 Ear covering

DOWN
1 Hefty competitor
2 French bread
3 Similar
4 Starfleet captain's declaration
5 More chichi
6 Former Giants player Jason
7 "Ol' Man River" composer
8 Holiday lead-ins
9 Very early
10 Captain of the Yankees
11 9mm guns
12 Body language expert?
13 Sonneteer, e.g.
19 Staff symbols
21 Contents of some bags
24 Club with clubs in its logo: Abbr.
25 Area of a ship where ceremonies take place
26 Game for wannabe multimillionaires
27 A long time
28 Prefix with structure
29 Keanu's "Matrix" role
30 "Rocky" character Apollo
31 Sirloin's section
32 Euchre player's declaration
37 Gifted traveler?
38 Cleveland NBAer
40 To such an extent
43 Bird's horn
47 Site
48 Paid attention
49 Struggle to make, with "out"
50 Particularly suitable place
52 Fifteen to
53 Kind of ski lift
54 London's ___ Gallery
55 Black
56 Kind of tide
57 Granduncle of Onan
58 Bureau of Prohibition notable
59 Hike
61 Atl. crosser, once

ANSWER, PAGE 95

62

THEMELESS 27

BY KAREN M. TRACEY

ACROSS

1 Whirlybirds
8 One-two's one
15 Oil alternative
16 Took in too much
17 More clamant
18 Last Supper room
19 Response: Abbr.
20 Comparable (with)
22 Schafskopf successor
23 Disdainful sound
25 Peppers
27 Not std.
28 Vocal sound
29 "Blues From the Rainforest" musician Saunders
30 Something that might make the fur fly?
32 Grammy-winning R&B album of 1987

34 Protected, in a way
36 Lillian Lust portrayer in "Bedazzled"
38 Like some parents
40 Barrymore and Waters
43 Yield (to)
44 Two-term governor and three-term senator from Nebraska
46 Isopyre, e.g.
47 Noncombat area: Abbr.
48 Less wavering
50 Cut back
51 Squirrelfish's habitat

53 Rival of 2000 Flushes
55 2005 batting champ Derrek
56 Carmaker Maserati
58 Up the creek
60 Rock and Roll Hall of Fame inductee category since 2000
61 It may fade in winter
62 Height
63 Treated with disdain

DOWN

1 Rummy variety
2 Alito's predecessor on the bench

3 1894 novel describing the adventures of Rudolf Rassendyll, with "The"
4 Heisman winner Detmer et al.
5 Posthumous Tony winner for "Cats"
6 Nothing, in Nice
7 Fix
8 Town ordinance
9 Turn inside out
10 Marsh
11 Refrain syllables
12 Plant of the arum family
13 On the lam
14 Visibly irate, maybe

21 Lost
24 Shoot over
26 Bony fish
29 Wailuku's island
31 Mainstay
33 Command center: Abbr.
35 Young voter
37 "___ Says I Love You" (1996 Woody Allen film)
38 Speak to
39 Bad mark in school
41 The inside track
42 Came down hard?
45 Circles, in a way
49 Arrant
50 Home of Perot Systems
52 Pump fillers
54 God slew him
57 Where Eric Dickerson played college ball
59 ___-mo

ANSWER, PAGE 81

63

PORK IT OVER

BY STEVE SALMON

ACROSS

1 Persian, for example
4 Annul, as a judgment
10 Full of enthusiasm
14 Seat, in slang
15 Site of the Great Sandy Desert
16 Costar of Dustin in "Tootsie"
17 Performer of a waggle dance
18 Neighboring schools, often
19 Kinkajou's home
20 56-Across for a tricky deception by author Stout, or a passage near the ER?
23 Twosomes
24 To the ___ degree
25 Nice place to learn
28 56-Across for a scarcity of animals, or April 22 in Oakland?
32 Olds of old
33 Elementary dog?
34 WWII leader
35 Draft members
38 Emile portrayer in Broadway's "South Pacific"
40 Stowe it?
43 Cut short
45 Take a dive?
49 56-Across for rubbish left by a prom partner, or a butt collector that needs to be cleaned fewer than four times a month?
53 Oscar-winning title role for Diane
54 Sharp competitor
55 Lane with the album "Be Mine Tonight"
56 Secret code, in the secret code
60 "Hell ___ no fury ..."
62 Rocker Dee Dee
63 Eggy quaff
65 Mallomar alternative
66 Lusters
67 ___ Appia
68 Yellow-card
69 Senior
70 On sick leave

DOWN

1 Tinker, Evers, or Chance, e.g.
2 Like some reproduction
3 1979 film directed by Mark Rydell
4 Be different
5 Richards of "Jurassic Park"
6 Hollow
7 Disconcerts
8 Hoe, perhaps
9 Apply less pressure, with "up"
10 Annex
11 See 60-Down
12 E.U. member
13 Pass on
21 Texas leaguer?
22 Damp
23 Operation Pipe Dreams org.
26 Stripling
27 Regard
29 Square dance?
30 Siamang, e.g.
31 Cartoonist Chast
36 Pass catcher
37 Long of "Soul Food"
39 Having half as many digits as hex
40 Word with dog or biscuit
41 Relative
42 Match, maybe
44 Structure in the Louvre courtyard
46 Pope whose election begat the Great Schism
47 Bottom topper?
48 Parliament call
50 Enthusiastic about
51 Broadway opening
52 Peter, Paul, and Mary, e.g.
57 Craft that located the Titanic in 1985
58 Dixie pronoun
59 Embed
60 With 11-Down, expression of wonder
61 Macaw's genus
64 Lass

ANSWER, PAGE 83

THEMELESS 28

BY WILL NEDIGER

ACROSS

1 Emulates Eddie "The Eagle" Edwards
9 Illegal search, in slang
15 From birth
16 Seat of New York's Tompkins County
17 Pencil wood
18 Sot
19 Wicket W. Warrick, for one
20 Thora Birch's "Ghost World" role
22 It might be piped into a mall
23 Ailurophile's purchase
25 Fire starter, maybe
26 Up
30 Attack first
32 1927 A.A. Milne book
34 Words said with one's right hand raised

37 Buckeye
38 ___ analysis (branch of calculus)
40 Smoking alternative
41 Trivial
45 General manager of the Red Sox
47 Zephyrinus and Zosimus, e.g.
48 Low-budget publication
50 Ready to go
52 Fear of Frankfurters?
54 Mood indicator, maybe
55 Olympic archer
59 Electrician's tool
61 Setting for many pickups

63 The senses, e.g.
64 The Mersey flows to it
65 Elite groups
66 Stay dry

DOWN

1 Bring into being
2 Had no doubts about
3 ___-Germanic
4 "Lord of the Flies" antagonist
5 Bear dance participant
6 Euripides tragedy
7 Pertaining to the sole of the foot
8 Hypodermic
9 Slobber stopper

10 Small matter?
11 They're spooky
12 Adds liveliness to something
13 Vast quantity
14 Hounds' sounds
21 Abode, informally
23 Routs
24 Lav
26 At once, once
27 Neighborhood next to Mayfair
28 Like some airplanes
29 Island invaded in 1945, for short
31 Immune
33 Hurricane name retired in 1977
35 Give medicine to

36 Some bank deposits
39 Talk like lovers
42 Sixer rival
43 Unit of information
44 Catch
46 Euro predecessor
48 "Ship Arriving Too Late to Save a Drowning Witch" rocker
49 Place of admission
51 Chilling
53 Coal porter?
55 Off-the-wall reaction?
56 Finish off the defense
57 Conscriptable
58 Notary public's need
60 '60s campus org. that protested the Vietnam War
62 Tupolev Tu-144 was the first one

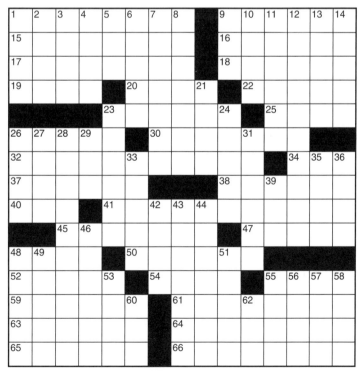

ANSWER, PAGE 85

"SWISH!"

BY JESSE GOLDBERG

ACROSS

1 Handles difficulties
6 Rent
10 Certain drawers
14 Queen, worker, or soldier, e.g.
15 Robbin' Robin
16 Longtime Miss America host Parks
17 Description of 30-Down, for most of his career
20 Advocate
21 6 letters
22 ___ lepton (physics particle)
23 Algerian city on the Mediterranean
25 Summerall contemporary
27 Alan Freed, for one
31 Best Musical the year "Children of a Lesser God" was Best Play
33 Knowledge base?
34 "___ F" (hit from "Beverly Hills Cop")
35 Grunge fan?
39 Dak., in the 1800s
40 Motherboard maker
41 Game with runners
42 Nailed
43 Auction actions
44 Backyard border

45 "32 Flavors" singer Davis
47 Dean of investing
48 Author of "The Two Cultures"
51 Fabrication
53 Cover subject of the April 1968 issue of Esquire
54 Codgers' replies
56 "Dunno"
61 Image embedded in the shaded squares of this puzzle, from 30-Down to the 26-Down
64 School that Ian Fleming (and James Bond) attended

65 Prevaricated
66 Sister-in-law of Jeb
67 Button with an envelope on it, perhaps
68 Event on a piste
69 Ohio natives

DOWN

1 Letters on the shirts of the losers of the Miracle on Ice
2 Setting of Haiku Gardens
3 Schrödinger equation letters
4 Make a lasting impression?
5 Bubbles seen at the beach

6 Birch of "American Beauty"
7 Express amazement
8 "Marvin's ___"
9 Katey Sagal's TV husband
10 Contents of some cartridges
11 Sports car that debuted in the '50s
12 "In a ___-nighted December ...": Keats
13 Olympic gymnast Kerri
18 Like Quentin Tarantino films
19 ___ l'Évêque (strong cheese)

24 Overnight
26 Part of 61-Across
27 Brent Spiner role
28 Organizational chart topper, for short
29 Dubliner's country
30 He made a famous 61-Across on June 14, 1998
32 Peacenik gestures
34 Partner for ever
36 Gave temporarily
37 With 59-Down, again
38 Huguenot descendant, perhaps
40 Not right now
44 Wangle
46 MGM cofounder Marcus
47 Royal Hospital Chelsea architect
48 Casino cashier confiners
49 Word with hot or home
50 Cowell with a scowl
52 Withstand
55 Bargain, to a Brit
57 Anastasia's father, e.g.
58 Water, in Chinese
59 See 37-Down
60 Flight deck calculations
62 Ultimate
63 Family tree word

ANSWER, PAGE 87

THEMELESS 29

BY JEFFREY HARRIS

ACROSS
1 Web feed
8 Movie whose title character is named Navin Johnson
15 Perennial "Christmas in Rockefeller Center" host
16 Quiche shunners, supposedly
17 Breathe
18 Coming
19 Enzyme suffix
20 Part of the Pentateuch
22 Día de ___ Muertos
23 Virile guy
25 Jerry's father on "Seinfeld"
26 Rattles
27 Pig in the Jim Davis comic strip "U.S. Acres"
29 Down Under hopper
30 Johnny's last "Tonight Show" guest
31 Birds
33 Worst off, in a way
35 "And ___!"

36 Team that beat Atl. in the 2001 NLCS
37 Flashes
41 Honorable behavior
45 Home of the Minoan civilization
46 Symbol of viscosity
48 Source of kerosene
49 Aoudads' dads
50 It may ring in the morning
52 Like some history
53 "Prince ___" ("Aladdin" song)
54 Island south of Martinique

56 Afflict
57 Government revenue source
59 Toddler's shout upon finishing a meal
61 Less of a mess
62 Puma, e.g.
63 Thoroughly enjoyed oneself, slangily
64 Neuter

DOWN
1 Shade provider
2 Substitute approved by the FDA in 1996
3 Creator of the Once-ler
4 Force unit?
5 Related

6 Hypo contents
7 They cause people to be on shaky ground
8 Bird's-eye view locale
9 Unit of inductance
10 Organs with drums
11 Distaff half of Bennifer
12 Model oneself after
13 Comebacks
14 Israeli parliament
21 "My man!"
24 Throw some back
26 Long Island town

28 Mythological Theban with a chemical element named after her
30 Underling of Fearless Leader
32 Rebus puzzle pronoun
34 Participate in crew
37 Use one's nails
38 Happy-go-lucky refrain
39 Like some soundtracks
40 "Casino Royale" star
41 Buzzard food
42 Offering of some bars
43 Noted New York City restaurant on Second Avenue
44 They have a lot of bills
47 Heaviest variety of lepton
50 Befuddled
51 "Mr. Pim Passes By" playwright
54 Gave evidence, maybe
55 Basketball Hall of Famer English
58 Sound heard while shearing
60 ___ Friday

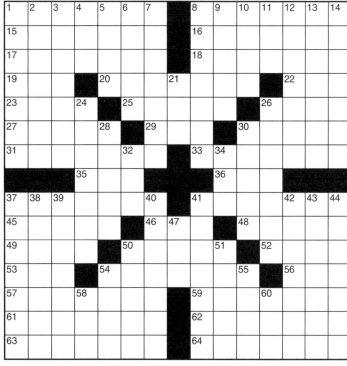

ANSWER, PAGE 89

SIGNS OF THE ...

BY TIMOTHY POWELL

ACROSS

1 Terminal
6 One-fifth of MMMXXV
9 Exposed
13 Kitchen magnet
14 Indignation
15 Oklahoma city
16 Often
18 Counterculture magazine
20 Spoonbill's relative
21 Pius IV's last name
23 Sound of relief
24 German pronoun
25 Englander
26 It's past due
27 Dickens novel
30 1989 R.E.M. hit
31 Unwrought iron
32 Anger
34 "Get lost!"
36 Burn slightly
38 Rock on the Hollywood Walk of Fame
39 South Pacific wraps
41 Cruising
42 Hello, in Portuguese
43 Focus on, in a way
45 TV schedule openings
49 Bag thickness unit
50 Precisely
52 Poetry Out Loud org.
53 Adam's apple source
54 Open
55 Squeals cats love to hear?
56 Shortcut
58 Marching bands often perform during them
60 Bathroom liner
61 Philips of "UHF"
62 Wrist-to-elbow bones
63 Little ___ Burdette (character in the "Smokey and the Bandit" movies)
64 Energy Policy Act of 2005 topic: Abbr.
65 Equals

DOWN

1 Starve
2 Horse source
3 More stylish
4 "___ View" (David Hare play)
5 Noted newspaper, in its Web address
6 Varied
7 Final line of a movie?
8 Motto of Harvard
9 Passé
10 Singer DiFranco with the album "Puddle Dive"
11 Ziti alternative
12 Sean Connery's costar in "The Rock"
17 Fed. fiscal agency
19 Payroll form
22 Ellipses, parabolas, etc.
28 Member of SPECTRE
29 Staff numbers
33 Host
35 Spoken
36 Have a Pavlovian response, perhaps
37 "Rosemary's Baby" author
39 Occasionally
40 Lit
41 Stuffed oneself
44 They start
46 Top-of-the-tenth score, perhaps
47 William Shatner sci-fi novel
48 Talks back to
51 2003 film directed by Jon Favreau
55 "The Real Thing" Tony winner Jennifer
57 "Strange Magic" group
59 "Drop your pencils!"

ANSWER, PAGE 91

THEMELESS 30

BY TRIP PAYNE

ACROSS
1 Brian Epstein fired him
9 Ultrahot masses
15 Phrase followed by "gratia plena"
16 Curl, as paint on a wall
17 Start of some sequel titles
18 "Taxi" driver Nardo
19 It's stuck in the grass
20 Like some sweaters
21 Monokini settings
26 Out-and-out
27 Battling
28 Dermatologist
30 Company owned by General Motors
34 Marathoners' concerns
35 Tag abbr.
36 Navel variety
37 Spinoff of 1980
38 Née follower
40 Opposite of matin
41 "Sunday in the Park With George" inspiration
42 Insatiable eaters, in slang
46 Dow Jones publication
47 Island ring
48 Connected, in a way
49 Shea manager
54 Van Helsing's creator
55 "Yada, yada, yada"
56 Building workers
57 Ortho product

DOWN
1 Course posting
2 Impending time
3 It's usually celebrated on the same day as Chinese New Year
4 Kangaroo Island creature, once
5 Slings Singapore slings, say
6 Argentine novelist Sábato
7 They might be bookmarked
8 Way out in China?
9 Alfresco
10 Instruction on a jukebox
11 Be at the head of the class
12 Parallel
13 Old characters
14 Set off the radar, perhaps
20 Killed, as a bill
21 Small sample
22 Debugging company?
23 Choice
24 They might merge
25 Barbara Gordon's other identity
29 Makes allegations
30 Rooster's cue
31 Company founded by Nolan Bushnell
32 Get a lock on
33 Ingredient in red flannel hash
36 Like a Möbius strip
38 Their ends are in sight
39 Magazine that produces an annual music festival
40 One who wouldn't mind finding roaches at home?
42 Xhosa, for example
43 Low deck
44 Wagon alternative
45 Give a thrill
46 Person with the biggest office, probably
49 Letters by a left-pointing arrow
50 Gambling locale: Abbr.
51 Itinerary portion
52 Backing
53 River to the Yangtze

ANSWER, PAGE 93

THE GRAVITY OF THE SITUATION

BY PATRICK JORDAN

ACROSS

1 Far from flashy
5 Eminent roster
10 Like a multiband receiver
14 Standout standing
15 Portaged item, often
16 FDR Memorial statue subject
17 Start of a produce department warning
20 Nut-flavored liqueur
21 Immature, in a way
22 "Catch ya later!"
23 Clarification lead-in
24 Bad way to go?
28 Pennsylvania and others: Abbr.
29 Starchy veggies
32 Starter of James Bond's car?
33 Made like a merino
35 A caddie might hold it

36 More of the warning
39 Up on the latest
40 1995 Jefferson portrayer
41 Beaten, in a way
42 Shout made with palms down
44 Rebuffing responses
45 Diet ruiners
46 Filibusterers, e.g.
48 Pinch
49 Medium-sized sofa
51 Fax forerunner
56 End of the warning
58 Viaduct supporter
59 Mohawk Valley city

60 Divas often have big ones
61 Towel inscription
62 Beeped
63 Beckinsale of "Serendipity"

DOWN

1 Backup contents
2 Extravagate
3 Composer of Carson's theme
4 "A History of the World in Six Glasses" drink
5 ___ chloride (dyemaking chemical)
6 Café order
7 An enthusiast of

8 Five-centime piece of old
9 Shawnee war chief
10 Brawl
11 Kabob preparer's activity
12 First three community cards in hold'em
13 Jerry Herman musical
18 Keanu Reeves's birthplace
19 Mo.-to-Me. direction
23 Steaming
24 Maze solutions, e.g.
25 Milo of "The Playboys"

26 Johnny Cash, to Carlene Carter
27 One in training pants
28 Canyoneering transports
30 Row
31 Likely finalists
33 Cords used as neckwear
34 Noise pollution unit
37 Forked over
38 Face, in slang
43 Inputs
45 Songfest offering
47 A caddy might hold it
48 Prepare for takeoff
49 10th grader, for short
50 Lake the Detroit River flows into
51 Bit of kindling
52 Tourist hike
53 Samadhi-seeker's discipline
54 Conspiracy
55 "If all ___ fails, read the directions"
57 Bus rte. stop

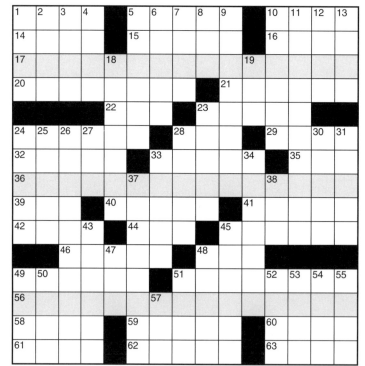

ANSWER, PAGE 95

70

THEMELESS 31

BY WILL NEDIGER

ACROSS

1 Sent up
8 Name that means "father of many"
15 More snappish
16 Howard Hawks's last film
17 License
18 Sign at a median break
19 Heal a heel?
20 Travelocity mascot
22 Mort's "Hi and Lois" partner
23 Superlatively aloof
26 Root word?
27 Obscure
28 Trig function
29 Three, they say
31 Exciting
32 "Good one!"
34 Pretty young things
35 Halloween cupcake decoration
37 Great deals

40 Daughter of Tony and Janet
44 Spanish province or its capital
45 Like some waste
46 Gp. whose members might greet each other with "What's up, doc?"
47 Parallel
48 ___ nobs (cribbage one-pointer)
49 Beer, in a boilermaker
51 Put coins in slots
52 Mocks
54 58-Down, in English
55 Make tight
57 Approve

60 Not yet there
61 Crackpots
62 Sterilized
63 Astrolabe descendant

DOWN

1 Like Absolut vodka
2 Nostrum
3 Leather source
4 Give one's view
5 Design school in NYC
6 Unagi or anago, e.g.
7 Undesirable part
8 Governor after Gray
9 Complex ecological community

10 Rake
11 Space neighbor
12 1953 film starring Tony Curtis and Janet Leigh
13 Shorten
14 Trifles (with)
21 "Fuhgeddaboud-it!"
24 Brown's creator
25 London vehicles
27 Command to a dealer
30 Contemporary of Faraday
31 Switzerland's most populous canton
33 Another time

34 Strip
36 Bikini line application
37 Was a strikebreaker
38 Words on a sample tray
39 Staff of Life
41 Valenzuela and Piazza's manager during their rookie seasons
42 Boston college
43 ___ money (contract confirmer)
45 Didn't stiff
48 Fashionable
50 Cancel
52 ___ Olympiques
53 Pulls some strings?
56 Playwright Akins
58 54-Across, in French
59 Fort ___ (Army base in New Jersey)

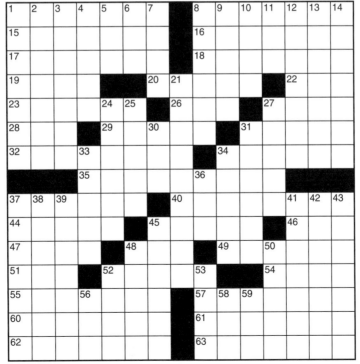

ANSWER, PAGE 81

SHORT PEOPLE

BY ROBERT H. WOLFE

ACROSS

1 Recessed section
5 Two-dimensional calculation
9 Certain sandwich
13 My brothel's keeper?
14 "Mamma Mia!" Tony nominee Ulvaeus
15 Billy of "The Phantom"
16 Defraud
17 Added without starting a new paragraph
18 Common conjunctions
19 Author of the children's book "The Blue Ribbon Day"
21 Delicacy
22 Chinese fruit
23 Car make named after an explorer
24 Cousins of pumas
26 Video shooter, for short

27 Recent
28 Seat of Indiana's Miami County
29 Crushed
32 "Laugh-In" regular
35 Cacti with edible fruit
37 Cold one
41 Show ender?
42 Get the chair
43 Part of TNT
46 Glorifies
48 Involuntary
49 Son of Iapetus
50 Actress in "Poseidon"
53 Backgammon impossibilities
54 Addiction
55 Make a mistake

57 Where kine dine
58 Inspiration for a troubadour
59 Giorgio rival
60 Past gas
61 Final four?
62 Egg holder

DOWN

1 They can be ripped
2 Cold floater
3 High fly catcher?
4 Character actress in "Ferris Bueller's Day Off"
5 Not flush with the wall, possibly
6 Pasta ___

7 A's third baseman Chavez
8 Naomi's "King Kong" role
9 Early Eurasian leaders
10 Pole position
11 Like nonvintage wine
12 Grant
14 Spread news of
20 "My, my!"
21 Cadence
22 Amputate, with "off"
23 Fish ladder locales
25 Level
26 "Farewell: thou ___ not teach me to forget": Romeo

30 P, to Pericles
31 "Alice Doesn't Live Here Anymore" Oscar winner
33 University whose mascot is Jumbo the elephant
34 They hold the mayo
35 Era of liberalization
36 Pinxter flowers, e.g.
38 Bend over backward?
39 Feuding sides
40 Become the other half of
41 Fab Four member
44 Former name of kodakgallery.com
45 "___ Diary" (Pia Pera novel)
47 Catcher for the Texas Rangers?
50 "Go West" name
51 Net sales locale?
52 Hotelier César
54 Chop
56 S.F. setting

ANSWER, PAGE 83

THEMELESS 32

BY DAVID J. KAHN

ACROSS

1 Fun partner
6 Relatively cool red giant
11 Neighbor of xenon on the periodic table
12 Ford model
14 Some moneylenders
17 Record players
18 Shrinks back
19 Potsdam pronoun
20 Slender shoe description
22 Sycophantic answers
23 Suitable
24 Harts' mates
26 Realistic video game, informally
27 Oklahoma city north-northwest of Oklahoma City
28 London theatre
30 Short miner

32 One with briefs, briefly
33 Novel with the character Dorothea Brooke
36 They might need to be massaged after being bruised
38 Call for help
39 Some Bach pieces
42 Spliced thing
43 Parlor type: Abbr.
45 Dietetic phrase
46 Climb
47 Garment with a flap
49 "Streamers" playwright
50 Great ending

51 Singer who was in "Blue in the Face"
53 Murdered "Godfather" character Greene
54 FDR's nickname for Al Smith
57 Childish comeback
58 In-box contents
59 Sirius star
60 Brawler, e.g.

DOWN

1 Movie for which Ian McKellen received a Best Actor nomination
2 Freddy of D.C. United
3 Catchall abbr.

4 ___-level
5 Fall Classic, with "the"
6 Child's play promoter?
7 Corporate department
8 Clumsy boats
9 One of Ptolemy's original 48 constellations
10 Is inheritable
11 Locked up
13 "Let's not go there"
14 Redfish Lake locale
15 Scoop
16 Grody, so to speak
21 Chief executive, at times

23 Power plant feature
25 Hockey Hall of Famer Abel
29 Components of some IRAs
31 Hockey Hall of Famer Neely
34 Regard
35 Actor Eldard of "House of Sand and Fog"
36 Snowy ___
37 Obi wearer
40 Things you shouldn't do
41 Take the conn
44 One who uses yeast
47 Deep sleep
48 Brand of cigar
51 Ex-
52 No-win situation
55 Riled (up)
56 Free from, with "of"

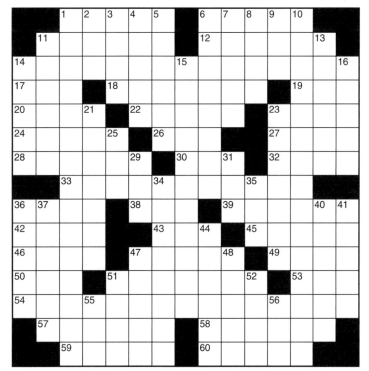

ANSWER, PAGE 85

FORWARD-LOOKING STATEMENT

BY SETH A. ABEL

ACROSS
1 Damage, so to speak
5 Went slowly
10 Specialists outrank them: Abbr.
14 Stickout
15 Glossy proof
16 Word on some European stamps
17 Particular
18 Less friendly
19 Apartment listing datum
20 With 60-Across, a quote by 38-Across
23 Hat with a tassel
24 AT&T Worldnet, for one
25 In recent times
27 NYU's business school
29 Cover letters?
32 Gold medalist at the 1984, 1988, 1992, and 1996 Olympics
33 Kick in
35 Dudgeon
37 IM provider
38 See 20-Across

43 Start of the second qtr.
44 Card
45 Good day?: Abbr.
46 Comic strip whose title character is named Sonya Hobbs
49 "Toodles"
51 Homecoming cry
55 Tarot deck division
57 Dune buggy, e.g.
59 It might be flat
60 See 20-Across
64 Outfielder Encarnación
65 Spring (from)
66 Return to sender?

67 Company that would be crazy to use the slogan "We never let you down"?
68 Wahhabi's faith
69 Diamond of note
70 Unibrowed Muppet
71 People's Sexiest Man Alive of 1992
72 They're found in many a yarn

DOWN
1 Palisades
2 Charger's home
3 Blackguard
4 After-dinner roll?
5 Steals

6 Game summaries
7 Like some poems
8 Class in which the teachers may be the only ones wearing underwear
9 What a bodysuit covers
10 "Nobody cares for eyes more than ___" (ad slogan)
11 "Shoot"
12 Genesis
13 Word with legs, chest, or palm
21 Caste member
22 Boston Patriots' org.

26 Green card holder's class, perhaps: Abbr.
28 Butt
30 Bespectacled "Lord of the Flies" boy
31 Away
34 Green coating
36 Wannabe dentist Hermey, e.g.
38 Expedition, for example
39 Quarterback's spot?
40 Golden alternative
41 Spin
42 Acumen
43 Dr.'s order?
47 Downtown sign
48 "Girls in Pants" author Brashares
50 Vexes
52 TV title role for Debra Messing
53 Five iron
54 Sings the praises of
56 "Encore!"
58 Motif
61 Estimate follower
62 Satisfying amount
63 Be in limbo
64 Gig

ANSWER, PAGE 87

THEMELESS 33

BY KAREN M. TRACEY

ACROSS
1 Happily
11 "The Art of Fugue" composer
15 Dissonant
16 ___-Tass
17 Summer camp activity
18 Special event rental
19 Government building
20 Magazine that Zigzag was a spinoff of
21 Directs
22 Constituency
23 Actor Cage, informally
26 Playwright Margolin
27 Bug
28 Book before Jarom in the Book of Mormon
30 Complicated process
32 Drubs
34 Amt.
35 "Civic Arousal" author
36 Costar of Dawn Wells
39 Flat flooring
40 Impose (upon)
41 Last Hebrew letter
43 Setting for Christmas in Connecticut: Abbr.
44 Five-time Super Bowl champs, briefly
45 Happy-go-lucky person's lack
47 Some Mille Bornes cards
48 Wait by the phone, perhaps
52 "House" actress Edelstein
53 Easy-to-park car
54 State with surety
55 Muddled
56 Cold War side
57 By some measure

DOWN
1 The Badger State: Abbr.
2 Grooving on
3 "Sweeter ___ You" (Ricky Nelson hit)
4 Astringent
5 Fought
6 More mean-spirited
7 Portuguese East Africa, today
8 They appear next to contract changes: Abbr.
9 Waiter's spot
10 Hosp. chart
11 Two-sided
12 1991 Traci Lords movie
13 Shooting equipment
14 Founder of EDS
20 Wimbledon winner before Lleyton
22 Enthusiasm
23 Topic of mechanics
24 Discouraging
25 Take attendance, perhaps
27 Stopping place
29 Junkyard find
31 Volkswagen model
33 Musical marks
37 "___ bodkins!"
38 Otalgia
42 Kills, as bills
45 25% of veinte
46 Common vacation destination
48 ___ Feiner
49 Start the bidding
50 "___ et manus" (MIT's motto)
51 "Symphony in Black" artist
53 Early year of the previous millennium

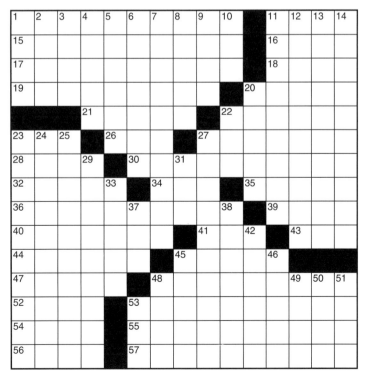

ANSWER, PAGE 89

ZOUNDS!

BY GARY STEINMEHL

ACROSS
1 Dope
5 5-Across, e.g.
9 ___-ply tire
13 Kindle
15 Move, in the real estate biz
16 Name of the baker in "The Godfather"
17 Sound of a snicker
18 Era alternative
19 Makeup kit item
20 What Egyptian marathoners might do?
23 Article in Le Figaro
24 Word with fire or water
25 Tool used to open a stuck jack-in-the-box?
29 Its emblem is a crescent
32 Male swans
33 NYC's A, B, C, or D
34 Emits
35 Brownie
36 Large luxury car?
38 Neighbor of Uru.

39 Washington State mascot
41 French ruler
42 Novello of "The White Rose"
43 "Strong of Heart: Life and Death in the Fire Department of New York" author Thomas Von ___
44 Hat worn at the Shriners' Christmas party?
46 Specially trained group
48 Acronymic title character of '80s TV
49 Put a dog on the grill?

54 Is up
55 Actual
56 Masada king
58 "Sacre ___!"
59 Barely beat
60 Yoga posture
61 Sylvester's problem
62 Refuse
63 Some Feds

DOWN
1 L.A. wintertime setting
2 Phone co. employee
3 Island with a state capital
4 Divorce law topics
5 Xena's horse
6 Swain

7 Fruit-filled pancake
8 Musical form with a refrain
9 What you will
10 Insert blank pages between
11 Hussein defense witness
12 Absorb, with "up"
14 He played Johnny in "Johnny Mnemonic"
21 Doctor
22 Non-NATO European country
25 Short-sleeved shirts with collars

26 Clouds
27 Part of DJIA
28 Eric's "Will & Grace" costar
30 Pollo accompanier
31 Rom. Catholic title
32 Grammy-winning gospel singer Winans
34 Colt of fame
36 Travel magazine advertiser
37 It lasts between four and five galactic years
40 Gets ready
42 Most doubtful
44 Break away
45 Symbol of angular acceleration
47 Party hearty
49 "Ha'i" land?
50 Cacoëthes
51 Peacock tail features
52 People mover
53 Raptors' defense, maybe
54 OPEC unit
57 Sex columnist Savage

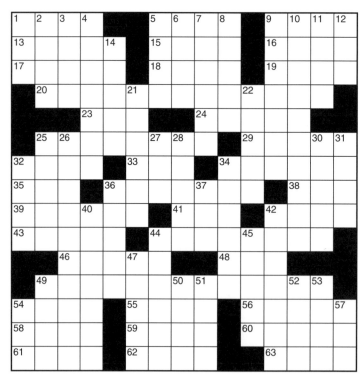

ANSWER, PAGE 91

THEMELESS 34

BY WILL NEDIGER

ACROSS

1 Legerdemain expert
9 Blame
15 Cosmetics ingredient
16 Emotionally distraught
17 Somewhat sharp, perhaps
18 Tags
19 i squared, then squared again
20 Record
21 Contemporary of Luciano
22 Bawean Island's setting
24 Sharp
25 Wernicke's ___ (part of the brain)
28 Dissect
30 Road block?
32 Don't keep the waiter waiting
36 "___ Goes Bananas" (1980 movie)
37 Cosmetics ingredient
38 Home to the Rhine-Westphalia Institute for Economic Research
39 Alioth is in it

42 Place for a party
44 See 3-Down
45 A tragic hero has one
48 "Ocean's Eleven" group
50 Roll-on alternative
52 Duran Duran album with the hit "Hungry Like the Wolf"
53 Section starter
56 Crimean War weapons
57 President of France during the early years of the Third Republic
59 Ophiologist's study

60 Not working
61 Sucrase, e.g.
62 Mark of a bad speaker

DOWN

1 Like some fatigues, for short
2 Huston's costar and fellow Best Supporting Actress nominee for "Enemies, A Love Story"
3 With 44-Across, part of a rocket
4 Spray
5 It hangs down from the soft palate
6 Overhaul

7 Herb in Italian dressing
8 Tubular
9 Gamboling
10 Royal Crown product
11 Ace
12 Liberate, maybe
13 Kid that's napped
14 Hewlett-Packard rival
21 Scorer of Brazil's 100th World Cup goal
22 "O frabjous day!" source
23 ___ Remo
25 Pine
26 Is contrite about

27 Shows one's humanity?
29 Video camera feature
31 0, for 180°
33 Karateka's workplace
34 Black, to Blake
35 Extraordinary
37 Negril native
39 Atyrau's river
40 Hogwash
41 Tony, for one
43 Stick with a net
45 Questionnaire choice
46 Grammy winner for Best Female Country Vocal Performance the year before Trisha
47 Ball handler?
49 Lock opener, informally
51 Have the look of being
53 "Vincent & ___" (1990 Robert Altman movie)
54 Color similar to mahogany
55 Ms. Pac-Man ghost
57 Crybaby's cry
58 Ravens owner Modell

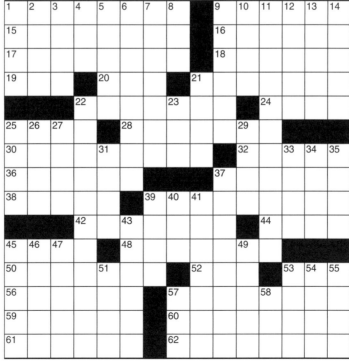

ANSWER, PAGE 93

77

OPENING PAIR

BY JACK McINTURFF

ACROSS

1 They grew up during the disco era, for short
5 Swear
8 What a Round Rock Express player may one day become
13 Roentgen's discovery
15 Balin of "The Patsy"
16 Mighty mount
17 Church figure
19 Heartsease, e.g.
20 Place for boarding
21 Holdups
22 Smell
23 Find by chance
25 Unmanned aircraft
27 Drunk
28 Feel sorrow
29 Window sticker
30 Divide into branches
32 One with a code name
33 Dealer's query, and what can precede the starts of 17-, 23-, 48-, and 57-Across
36 DoctorFinder org.
39 Like presses
40 Make aware

45 Memoir that preceded "Teacher Man"
46 XXXV × XL
47 Canonical hour recitation
48 Like a forceful leader
52 Inverno precipitation
53 Lover of Arthurian legend
54 Cause for a trip to the pediatrician, perhaps
56 Debussy contemporary
57 Math major's class
59 At attention
60 Forum greeting

61 Stopped lying?
62 Game with a board that has 82 distinct sections
63 Referendum choice
64 Slant

DOWN

1 Really big, on a label
2 Mark of a mistake
3 Former owner of the San Diego Padres
4 2005 film for which George Clooney won the Best Supporting Actor Oscar

5 VJ part
6 Late bedtime
7 It's good for "absolutely nothing," according to a 1970 #1 hit
8 Look
9 ___-climber (gym apparatus)
10 Some muscles
11 Gets some shuteye
12 Great adventure
14 Host
18 Discharges between electrodes
21 Short poem
22 Sum
24 TV toon boy

26 Marrero of the Mets
30 Actor on a 2005 postage stamp
31 1981 sitcom honeymoon locale
34 Cranny
35 Smoke solids
36 Clad
37 Matthew Broderick's "Ferris Bueller's Day Off" costar
38 Invite for a playdate, e.g.
41 Some cavalry soldiers
42 Simple locking gadget
43 Football play
44 Hip-sounding Green Day drummer ___ Cool
46 Former Golden Arches sandwiches
47 Smart
49 A-list
50 "Switching Channels" costar
51 February 2005 Central Park display, with "The"
55 "So that's where I left it!"
57 For instance
58 Fine-grained wood

ANSWER, PAGE 95

7 THEMELESS 1

```
W E B B R O W S E R ■ O L I N
O P E R A H O U S E ■ C A N A
N O N O N S E N S E ■ C U S S
■ S E M I ■ ■ T A L M U D I C
■ ■ ■ S T R A Y ■ A R E N A ■
D E C K ■ H A N S O N ■ R U R
A Q U A T I C S ■ D O O D A D
N U R T U R E ■ F E R M A T A
C A V O R T ■ T A S S E L E D
E T E ■ B Y W A Y S ■ N E S S
D I T T O ■ I L E A C ■ ■ ■
R O T O T I L L ■ ■ A L A S ■
A N I N ■ S L I D E R U L E S
M A N Y ■ L I E U T E N A N T
A L G A ■ A S S I S T A N T S
```

17 THEMELESS 5

```
A A R O N S O R K I N ■ V C R
T R A V E L G U I D E ■ E R A
U S M E D A L I S T S ■ S O S
N E A R ■ P E N T A T E U C H
E N D U P ■ ■ G S E V E N ■
■ E A S E D ■ B U S ■ R I T E
■ ■ E R O T I C ■ T O U T S ■
C I T ■ K E E B L E R ■ S I S
A R A B Y ■ A L A N I S ■ ■
M O P E ■ A L E ■ S P A S M ■
O N E E G G ■ ■ E B E R T ■
M O N T R E A L E R ■ R A M A
I R A ■ O N A U T O P I L O T
L E D ■ S T A T E S E N A T E
E S E ■ Z S A Z S A G A B O R
```

27 THEMELESS 10

```
S T J A M E S ■ A G A T E S ■
T R A B E R T ■ P R E T E X T
R E V E L R Y ■ A T L A N T A
A V E ■ ■ E X O T I C ■ S E R
F I L M E D ■ W R E A K E R S
E N I A C ■ D E O ■ P L U N K
D O N C H E A D L E ■ U P S Y
■ ■ B O N N ■ C E L T ■ ■
F L E E ■ G Q M A G A Z I N E
L I N T S ■ U A R ■ L E N O X
I N T H E W A Y ■ T O S S U P
P E E ■ R I Y A D H ■ T V A
T A R B E L L ■ M E A L I E R
O R I E N T E ■ A S T O L A T
P A N D A S ■ ■ J E T B L U E
```

37 THEMELESS 15

```
S I T O N I T ■ J E T S K I S
A T H L E T E ■ E X O T I C A
N E E D H A M ■ R I D D L E S
I R R ■ I L P O S T O ■ D O H
B A E R ■ Y E S E S ■ J A V A
E T S E Q ■ S L Y ■ C A R E Y
L E A D U P T O ■ G O N E R S
■ ■ Z E U S ■ C U R E ■ ■
A S K O U T ■ D O N E D E A L
V H O N E ■ I E R ■ D O N N A
E I N E ■ K N A P P ■ E T A T
N A T ■ L A N D S A T ■ W H O
U T I L I Z E ■ M A R R I E S
E S K I M O S ■ A V I O N I C
Q U I Z N O S ■ N O X Z E M A
```

8 TURNING STATE'S EVIDENCE

```
R U I Z   H A R M S   L A C K
I N G E   A R U B A   A B L E
D I O R A M A B A L A N C E R
S T R O L L B Y     V I S O R
      I I I     C M O N
O W I N G N I M O Y W A G E S
S A L O N   S A M M S   I D O
A K I N   L O O P Y   G R I P
K E A   S A B R E   N O T C H
A N D E A N A I D N I G H T S
      A J A R     A X E
E X T R A   D E M O T A P E
D R U N K R O Y W E N T M A D
G A B E   O W N E R   E M M Y
E Y E D   B L E S S   R O S S
```

18 THREE FROM THE BIG TEN

```
M I D A S   T A L C   S L U R
A D O R N   O L A Y   E A S E
R O C C O   P I M P E R N E L
      H O O S I E R D A D D Y
A M B I T S   R U G   I T O
R O A M   A M P   S I G N O N
M A N E   G O A T   E R G
  B A D G E R C O U R A G E
  N E E   K E R N   Y E A R
B E A S T S   R E P   M A S T
I R S   S P A   E C A R T E
G O P H E R N A U G H T
M I L I T A N T S   A T E A M
A C I D   W I T S   M E T R O
C A T E   L E A R   P R A T T
```

28 HIDDEN SEASONAL SIGNS

```
S T O P   B R A N D   D E L L
L A V A   R E S E E   O R E O
A P E R   A V I A N   T I N T
V E R T I G O A T T A C K S
      T A S K     U F O
B E D I M   E X T R A M A Y O
A B O M B   H O E R   L O W
S O R E   R O O T S   B A K E
A N I   B I A S   W O M E N
L Y C R A B R A S   I D O L S
      A R C   I S P Y
  T R I B A L A N C E S T O R
J O A N   G O U G E   L A Z Y
O O Z E   E A T E N   A D Z E
B L E D   S N O R E   M A Y S
```

38 HAMMING IT UP

```
E G A D   O P T S   S H R U B
P A R R   C A S A   M O U S E
O R C A   E T A L   O R G A N
X R A Y H A R R I S O N
Y E N   O N O   V O T E F O R
  T A L K I N G A S H T R A Y
    S E A   O R O   A H A
B I D D Y   B L Y   B B G U N
O N E   F L A   M U M
S T E V I E U N D E R W A Y
E L M O N T E   R A N   V I A
  O L E C O U N T R I E S
H O R D E   H O N E   I D L Y
I D I O T   I N K S   O L D E
M E M O S   P A S T   S Y S T
```

47 THEMELESS 20

```
B L A S T E R S ■ P A R R O T
E A R C A N A L ■ I G U A N A
F U M A N C H U ■ N A T I C K
E R A T ■ R A M J E T ■ N E E
L I D ■ V U L P I N E ■ D O H
L E A S E S ■ G U S T A V E
■ U N T W I S T ■ A T E E
E G R E T ■ A R A ■ S N E R D
L A I D ■ C R E W M A N
E M P E R O R ■ C H A S M S
G E O ■ E Y E B A L L ■ H E H
A B S ■ B O D E G A ■ K A T E
N I T W I T ■ L A R A I D E R
C R E O L E ■ O P E N D O O R
E D S E L S ■ W E N T A W R Y
```

55 THEMELESS 24

```
S P A D E R ■ M I S S I L E
L U N A T E ■ V E N T U R E D
I T C H E S ■ E M E R G I N G
P S I ■ R E T R O ■ E A S Y A
A T L A N T A N ■ H A R H A R
D O L C E ■ L A R A M S ■
I S A T ■ I L L U S E ■ I A N
S E R V I C E E N T R A N C E
K A Y ■ R I S Q U E ■ I D E D
■ S E N T U P ■ F L O S S
R A G T A G ■ I T S A S N A P
E R R O L ■ I N O I L ■ E T A
I T A L I A N O ■ G L A S E R
C I T I Z E N X ■ N O R I S K
H E A D E R S ■ S W E A T S
```

63 THEMELESS 27

```
C O P T E R S ■ L E F T J A B
A C R Y L I C ■ O V E R A T E
N O I S I E R ■ C E N A C L E
A N S ■ O N A P A R ■ S K A T
S N O R T ■ P E L T S ■ I R R
T O N E ■ M E R L ■ M A N G E
A R E T H A ■ P A T E N T E D
■ R A Q U E L W E L C H
A D O P T I V E ■ E T H E L S
D E F E R ■ E X O N ■ O P A L
D M Z ■ S U R E R ■ P R U N E
R E E F ■ T Y D B O L ■ L E E
E R N E S T O ■ I N A S P O T
S I D E M E N ■ T A N L I N E
S T A T U R E ■ S N O O T E D
```

71 THEMELESS 31

```
S P O O F E D ■ A B R A H A M
W A S P I E R ■ R I O L O B O
E N T I T L E ■ N O U T U R N
D A R N ■ G N O M E ■ D I K
I C I E S T ■ O L E ■ H I D E
S E C ■ C R O W D ■ Z I N G Y
H A H A H A H A ■ C U T I E S
■ G U M M Y W O R M ■
S T E A L S ■ J A M I E L E E
C A D I Z ■ T O X I C ■ A M A
A K I N ■ H I S ■ C H A S E R
B E T ■ J A P E S ■ B O R N
B O O Z E U P ■ E N D O R S E
E N R O U T E ■ W E I R D O S
D E S E X E D ■ S E X T A N T
```

9 MARCH MADNESS

```
S H A Q | M C J O B | | J E T
O A H U | A R O M A | H O P I
S H E A | D A N N Y | A V I D
| A M Y N A M E I S A L I C E
| L U M P S | | G L A S S
C A M E L | | C L O W N |
A W E | L I T T L E | A M F M
L O G E | W O M E N | Y O R E
F L A Y | A L C O T T | O A T
| L E A S E | | A U N T S
O D I S T | | P A I R S
B E T H L E H E M S T E E L
E C H O | M O R A L | D D A Y
S K I T | M A I Z E | T A K E
E S C | A X L E S | O M E N
```

19 THEMELESS 6

```
E P I S C | T O M H A Y D E N
S A S H A | A N T I N O I S E
P I L E D | S T A N D U P T O
O N E D I M E | D E G |
| O Z A R K S | S O R T A
T U R N | I S A A C | T E R R
I S E E I T | T R U S T S I N
L E G H O R N | A R C H I V E
E N G I N E E R | S H A D E S
R E A M | D R A C O | T E T S
S T E W S | D E A R E R |
| R A S | N Y T I M E S
J A S O N K I D D | A G A P E
I D E N T I C A L | T H R E E
M A N G A N E S E | S T E E D
```

29 THEMELESS 11

```
C H E W B A C C A | C E D A R
R O Y R O G E R S | A L O N E
I N E E D A N A P | M A G N A
S K I N | S T E P | M C M L
T E N S E D | E R I C | H A I
O R G | L A N D S C A P E R S
| D E V O | I K N O W I T
| S T R A I N | O S M O S E
U N H A N D S | N O I R
N E W C O L O S S U S | T D S
S E A | R O L O | T S T R A P
E R R S | W U S S | H I Y A
A S T A R | B O O G I E B O Y
T A E B O | L O U I S I A N E
S T R U M | E N S N A R L E D
```

39 THEMELESS 16

```
I R O N C L A D S | C L I N G
S E R I A L M O M | H A M E L
L A S T S C E N E | I N A W E
E R O S I O N A L | P A G E S
| N O D | T A S T E R S
P I S T O L | | T H U |
A B L E | J U S T F O R M E N
R E A R M | A K A | T N O T E
E X T R A F R I E S | E R A S
| E D U | O G R E S S
Q U A V E R S | L U I
U N S E R | P L U R A L I Z E
A M O R E | E U M E N I D E S
Y E N T A | C R E S T L E S S
S T E E L | K E N T S T A T E
```

48 WANNA BET A SILK PAJAMA?

```
A L L P R O . G A M . S N A G .
D O O H A N . A S A . H A Z E .
O A X A C A . O Y L . I M A N .
. . . T H R I L L L A M A R R .
A B S . E O N . U R N . T I E .
R E C A L L L A M A N C H A . .
F L A X . L A T . T I A . . . .
S T R I P . W O K . E R R O L .
. . O A S . L A B . O O Z E .
. N U M S K U L L L A M A Z E .
S O N . T I P . E O S . N Y S .
T H R E E L L L A M A . . . . .
L I E S . L O O . T A T A M I .
E T A S . E A T . E R O D E D .
O S L O . T D S . D A Z Z L E .
```

56 X OUT

```
P O S E . A C R E . U T T E R .
E R O S . D U E L . C R A V E .
S E W S . D E L I . L I K E D .
O O H E D . S I X L A N E . .
. A X I S . V I A . K A T T .
B L T . N A D I R S . E C H O .
R O E . G R I N . E T H E L .
A W L . H A N G T E N . A R E .
Z E S T Y . T O M B . N E D .
O L E O . G O H O M E . C F O .
S L I P . A X E . A R T E .
. S C H L E P S . G R O W S .
C A N O E . Y A W N . I N R E .
C L E A R . E S A I . A M E X .
S A W T O . S T Y X . D E N Y .
        T       E       N
```

64 PORK IT OVER

```
C A T . V A C A T E . A V I D .
U S H . A R A B I A . T E R I .
B E E . R I V A L S . T R E E .
. X R A Y A I S L E W A Y . .
D U O S . N T H . E C O L E .
E A S T B A Y E A R T H D A Y .
A L E R O . S P O T . D D E .
. . O X E N . E Z I O . . . .
S K I . S N I P . S C U B A .
E I G H T D A Y A S H T R A Y .
A N N I E . R C A . A B B E .
. I G P A Y A T I N L A Y . .
H A T H . R A M O N E . N O G .
O R E O . G L I N T S . V I A .
W A R N . O L D E S T . I L L .
```

72 SHORT PEOPLE

```
A P S E . A R E A . C L U B .
B A W D . B J O R N . Z A N E .
S C A M . R A N I N . A N D S .
. K T C O U R I C . T R E A T .
L I T C H I . D E S O T O .
O C E L O T S . C A M . N E W .
P E R U . T R A M P L E D .
. R T J O H N S O N . .
. S A G U A R O S . B R E W .
B I Z . F R Y . T O L U E N E .
E X A L T S . F O R C E D .
A T L A S . M E R O S S U M .
T I E S . H A B I T . T R I P .
L E A S . E R A T O . Y V E S .
E S S O . W X Y Z . N E S T .
```

Q	A	N	T	A	S			G	R	A	N	A	D	A
A	R	A	R	A	T			R	A	B	B	L	E	S
T	E	R	E	S	A		A	I	R	B	A	L	L	S
A	N	N	E		Y	A	M	M	E	R		S	U	E
R	A	I	S	A		R	A	Y	S		S	P	I	N
I	S	A		V	E	R	N		T	A	O	I	S	T
			S	O	L	I	D	S		M	A	C	E	S
		D	I	C	K	V	A	N	D	Y	K	E		
F	O	R	T	E		E	B	E	R	T	S			
A	L	C	O	T	T		E	L	I	A		T	E	A
S	E	A	N		E	L	A	L		N	A	H	U	M
C	A	R		H	E	A	R	S	T		L	E	G	O
I	N	T	R	E	P	I	D		A	D	A	G	E	S
S	N	E	E	R	E	R		R	O	M	A	N	O	
M	A	R	S	R	E	D		T	R	O	P	E	Z	

L	A	P	S		R	A	M	✈		F	O	N	D	A
E	U	R	O		E	T	C	H		T	R	E	A	D
A	R	A	B		G	E	A	R		D	A	W	N	S
R	A	T	E		G	A	T	O		I	C	Y		
✈	S	T	R	E	A	M		T	A	X	L	O	S	S
		E	N	E		O	U	R		E	R	M	A	
D	E	E	R	E		F	L	I	P		K	I	T	
U	R	L		M	O	D	U	L	A	R		✈	L	I
K	I	R		Y	V	E	S		O	L	S	E	N	
E	C	O	L		A	R	E		A	P	E			
S	A	Y	A	B	L	E		O	B	✈	D	A	R	T
	✈	T	A		K	A	V	A		G	E	E	R	
A	S	S	E	S		✈	S	E	T		E	R	G	O
F	L	O	S	S		E	I	R	E		R	I	A	L
T	O	N	T	O		R	A	T	S		S	E	L	L

G	T	O	S		A	T	W	A	R		C	Z	A	R
N	E	H	I		P	H	O	T	O		R	I	L	E
A	C	I	D		P	O	R	T	O		E	T	O	N
W	H	O	E	V	E	R	N	A	M	E	D	I	T	
		B	A	A		C	I	A	O					
M	A	B		C	R	A	S	H	E	S		S	P	F
S	C	A	R		O	N	E		Y	A	H	O	O	
N	E	C	K	I	N	G	W	A	S	A	P	O	O	R
B	L	O	O	D		U	K	E		B	O	L	T	
C	A	N		T	O	S	P	A	R	E		T	S	E
		A	A	R	P		E	T	S					
J	U	D	G	E	O	F	A	N	A	T	O	M	Y	
T	U	N	A		L	U	I	G	I		O	D	I	E
S	N	I	P		S	T	R	U	T		L	O	L	A
K	E	T	T		E	S	S	A	Y		I	R	K	S

Z	Z	[TOP]		H	E	A	P			E	R	G		
A	A	H		F	O	S	S	I	L		T	A	I	
R	N	A		I	M	P	A	L	A		C	I	N	C
F	E	T	T	L	E		P	E	S	T		L	G	A
		I	T	E	M		S	T	R	E	W	E	R	
		P	R	E	C	I	S		L	A	M	A	R	R
[TIP]	P	L	E	R		N	A	S	A		B	Y	N	O
O	R	A		[TIP]	[TOP]	S	H	A	P	E		C	U	T
N	I	N	A		S	K	I	T		F	L	A	T	[TOP]
E	N	T	I	R	E		B	E	G	F	O	R		
I	T	A	L	I	C	S		D	R	E	G			
L	O	T		P	R	A	Y		A	N	Y	H	O	W
L	U	R	K		E	D	M	O	N	D		O	P	A
	T	E	E		T	A	H	I	T	I		T	U	X
S	E	N		T	A	S	S			[TIP]	S	Y		

49 THEMELESS 21

A	L	S		A	B	B	E		A	D	O	R	E	S
S	O	U	L	F	O	O	D		L	A	K	O	T	A
C	A	P	I	T	A	L	G	A	I	N	S	T	A	X
H	D	T	V				I	D	E	S		T	I	E
			E	A	S	T	E	R	N		M	E	L	S
I	N	S	I	N	C	E	R	E		P	I	N		
T	E	E	N	I	E	R		M	A	R	X	I	S	M
S	A	L	M	O	N			D	E	E	D	E	E	
A	T	L	A	N	T	A		Y	E	S	D	E	A	R
		S	I	S		S	T	A	L	E	M	A	T	E
A	B	C	D		I	T	E	R	A	T	E			
D	O	H		P	O	R	E			D	I	M	E	
D	R	E	S	S	T	O	T	H	E	N	I	N	E	S
L	A	A	L	A	A		H	A	V	E	A	G	A	S
E	X	P	A	T	S		E	T	A	T		E	L	O

57 THEMELESS 25

	S	D	A	K		U	M	A	S	S		B	I	C
	N	O	R	A		S	A	S	H	A		A	M	Y
F	O	G	G	Y	B	O	T	T	O	M		S	O	B
A	C	T	U	A	L		S	O	W		S	E	G	O
G	O	A	S	K	Y	O	U	R	M	O	T	H	E	R
E	N	G		S	T	P		S	E	A	R	I	N	G
N	E	S	S		H	U	B			F	A	T	E	S
		A	C	E	S	A	T	E	S	T				
A	B	A	T	E		T	U	X		A	C	N	E	
S	E	N	O	R	A	S		B	U	D		L	O	A
F	L	O	U	N	D	E	R	E	D	A	B	O	U	T
A	L	I	T		D	E	A		E	R	E	S	T	U
R	I	N		S	U	N	N	Y	S	I	D	E	U	P
A	N	T		A	C	I	D	S			N	E	B	R
S	I	S		L	E	N	D	L		G	W	Y	N	

65 THEMELESS 28

S	K	I	J	U	M	P	S		B	A	G	J	O	B
I	N	N	A	T	E	L	Y		I	T	H	A	C	A
R	E	D	C	E	D	A	R		B	O	O	Z	E	R
E	W	O	K		E	N	I	D		M	U	Z	A	K
			C	A	T	N	I	P		L	E	N	S	
A	S	T	I	R		A	G	G	R	E	S	S		
N	O	W	W	E	A	R	E	S	I	X		I	D	O
O	H	I	O	A	N			V	E	C	T	O	R	
N	O	N		M	I	C	K	E	Y	M	O	U	S	E
		E	P	S	T	E	I	N		P	O	P	E	S
Z	I	N	E		A	L	L	S	E	T				
A	N	G	S	T		T	O	N	E		E	R	O	S
P	L	I	E	R	S		B	A	R	S	C	E	N	E
P	E	N	T	A	D		I	R	I	S	H	S	E	A
A	T	E	A	M	S		T	E	E	T	O	T	A	L

73 THEMELESS 32

	G	A	M	E	S		S	S	T	A	R			
	I	O	D	I	N	E		T	A	U	R	U	S	
I	N	D	U	S	T	R	I	A	L	B	A	N	K	S
D	J	S		C	R	I	N	G	E	S		S	I	E
A	A	A	A		Y	E	S	E	S		R	I	P	E
H	I	N	D	S		S	I	M			E	N	I	D
O	L	D	V	I	C		D	O	C		A	T	T	Y
		M	I	D	D	L	E	M	A	R	C	H		
E	G	O	S		S	O	S		M	O	T	E	T	S
G	E	N	E			O	T	B		N	O	F	A	T
R	I	S	E		S	K	O	R	T		R	A	B	E
E	S	T		L	O	U	R	E	E	D		M	O	E
T	H	E	H	A	P	P	Y	W	A	R	R	I	O	R
	A	R	E	T	O	O		E	M	A	I	L	S	
	S	T	E	R	N		R	O	W	D	Y			

11 THE LAST GOODBYE

```
A B C ■ E O N ■ T I N A ■ ■ ■ ■
R A H ■ T B A ■ O V E R S E E ■
E R R ■ H I G H P I T C H E D ■
A N I T A ■ S A L E S ■ O R A ■
■ ■ S U N B A K E D ■ P R I M ■
L O T T ■ S T U V ■ T O T E S ■
P R I O R I ■ N E P H E W ■ ■ ■
G L A R E D ■ A L A R ■ A H A ■
A Y N ■ S E A M ■ W O L V E S ■
■ ■ S I E S T A ■ N B A E R S ■
S P L A T ■ M T G E ■ T R O T ■
C R A M ■ A C A D E M I A ■ ■ ■
R E T ■ P L A T A ■ I N D E X ■
A G E N T O R A N G E ■ I B M ■
G O R O U N D ■ S E N ■ O R E ■
■ ■ ■ W I G S ■ K O S ■ S O N ■
```

21 THEMELESS 7

```
S T R A P P E D F O R C A S H
E M O T I O N A L R E S C U E
G E T A L L I N A L A T H E R
A N S ■ C O G ■ T E D ■ E T A
■ ■ ■ S H I M ■ T A S K ■ ■ ■
N E A T A S A P I N ■ I M A C
A L B E R T ■ E R S ■ L U L L
O V O I D ■ M A E ■ M O N D O
M E I N ■ S E C ■ A U B R E Y
I S L E ■ E L E V A T I O N S
■ ■ ■ M O A T ■ E M I T ■ ■ ■
R E P ■ N C O ■ G I N ■ A M A
U S E D C A R S A L E S M A N
S T P A U L M I N N E S O T A
T H E D E F E N S E R E S T S
```

31 THEMELESS 12

```
S P A R E B E D ■ ■ J A S O N
T A X O N O M I C ■ U L T R A
A L L O C A B L E ■ S L O B S
T E E T O T A L S ■ T E N E T
■ ■ ■ ■ R E T ■ T R A G E D Y
G I L B E R T S ■ U F O ■ ■ ■
N O E L ■ S L U M B E R E R S
A T E U P ■ E P A ■ W I L E S
T A K E O R D E R S ■ S I F T
■ ■ ■ S O Y ■ S C H A T Z I S
B E N T L E Y ■ O A T ■ ■ ■
A Q U A S ■ A P P R O V A L S
T U T T I ■ P H O E N I C I A
H A T E D ■ S I L I C O N E S
E L Y S E ■ Z O N E L E S S
```

41 THEMELESS 17

```
D E T E R ■ G E E S E ■ A D S
E L E V A T O R C A R ■ E R A
B R E E Z E A L O N G ■ G E L
I O U ■ E X P E L ■ S W E A T
T Y P O ■ T E N E T ■ H A M M
■ ■ ■ B O S O M ■ U B A N G I
T A P I R ■ V E S T A ■ S I N
I L L T A K E Y O U T H E R E
T H E ■ R O R E M ■ H E A L S
L E N S E S ■ R E L E E ■ ■ ■
E D I E ■ S O F T Y ■ P O M P
R I T E S ■ S L I D E ■ P I E
O S U ■ I T S A M I R A C L E
L O D ■ R A I S E A S T I N K
E N E ■ S E E K S ■ T E T E S
```

50 ONE STEP AT A TIME

```
H O R I Z O N ■ A M O E B A S
O K I N A W A ■ C A N N O L I
T R A C I N G ■ T R E C O O L
■ A L [LOVE] R ■ W I T ■ [LAVE] R N E
■ ■ R E D R O V E R ■ S E X ■
M O S ■ ■ O A R ■ N A P ■ ■
I R T ■ S L I D ■ S W E A T Y
A C A P P E L L A ■ E E R I E
T A H O E ■ S A G E G R E E N
A S L E E P ■ D O G G ■ N U T
■ M C I ■ D N A ■ A P E
D A D ■ H O N E Y D E W ■
I S O [LATE] ■ N O R ■ C[HATE]A U
S P U R R E R ■ P R O V E R B
K I L A U E A ■ V A L E R I E
S C A L E R S ■ T H E R O S E
```

58 HOLLYWOOD SQUARES

```
G U T ■ M G M ■ ■ L A S E
A S H ■ 4 Y E A R ■ T H E U S
B E E ■ J R O T C ■ H A R P S
■ W E A R S ■ C A E S A R ■
S M I R C H ■ H O T W A T E R
K U L I K ■ R A L P H ■ E M U
A D D ■ S A U N A ■ O L S E N
■ 1 N A M E D ■ E L I ■
■ E N O ■ S W E E T 16
D I C E D ■ B A C K 9 ■ C A L
E C O ■ A V O W S ■ Y E A T S
B E L L J A R S ■ P A W N E D
■ B L A I N E ■ D A R E D ■
W E I L L ■ A C R I D ■ L E T
M E D A L ■ L O O N S ■ E R A
D R E W ■ ■ O P T ■ S E X
```

66 "SWISH!"

```
C O P E S ■ T O R E ■ B V D S
C A S T E ■ H O O D ■ B E R T
C H I C A G O H O O P S T E R
P U S H F O R ■ M N O ■ T A U
■ O R A N ■ E N B E R G
D E E J A Y ■ E V I T A ■
A X I O M ■ A X E L ■ S L O B
T E R R ■ I N T E L ■ K E N O
A C E D ■ N O D S ■ F E N C E
■ A L A N A ■ W I T T E R
C P S N O W ■ Y A R N ■
A L I ■ E H S ■ B E A T S M E
G A M E W I N N I N G S H O T
E T O N ■ L I E D ■ L A U R A
S E N D ■ E P E E ■ E R I E S
```

74 FORWARD-LOOKING STATEMENT

```
C O S T ■ C R E P T ■ P F C S
L U L U ■ R E P R O ■ E I R E
I T E M ■ I C I E R ■ A R E A
F L A S H B A C K S A R E A ■
F E Z ■ I S P ■ O F L A T E
S T E R N ■ S P F ■ L E W I S
■ A D D ■ I R E ■ A O L
S A M U E L G O L D W Y N
A P R ■ W A G ■ F R I
M O M M A ■ B Y E ■ I T S M E
A R C A N A ■ A T V ■ T A X
T H I N G O F T H E P A S T
J U A N ■ A R I S E ■ E C H O
O T I S ■ I S L A M ■ N E I L
B E R T ■ N O L T E ■ D Y E S
```

12 ONE MAN OUT

```
I D O N T █ █ A D D S █ W H O
N A N C E █ █ N O E L █ E O N
T U S C A N █ T O M O R R O W
O P T █ R U N █ R O T U N D A
W H A T █ N A B S █ █ H E I R
N I G H █ S U E █ B A R R E D
█ N E U █ █ S C A R F █ S S S
█ █ G I V E A D A R N █ █ █ █
M I S █ L U A U S █ █ I R S █
I M P A L E █ S O D █ C E N T
S P A N █ H E R E █ K N O W █
T E S T A T E █ B B Q █ A W E
B A S E B A L L █ T R O M P E
O C K █ E X P O █ S H E E T █
W H Y █ L I S T █ T O D A Y █
```

22 FASHION STATEMENT

```
█ J I B █ O P E C █ G O B A D
D O R A █ R U N E █ I N A N E
I N O R D E R T O █ B E R G S
M I N N E L L I █ B E A T E R
█ M A A S █ T R A █ D A L E █
B E I R R E P L A C E A B L E
B A N D █ R E C O P Y █ █ █ █
C U E █ T H E █ I N A █ O L D
█ █ S H A S T A █ █ E B A Y █
O N E M U S T A L W A Y S B E
N E V E █ P O R █ O L E O █ █
S W E L L S █ N I L E B L U E
P I N T O █ D I F F E R E N T
E S S E N █ E S S E █ O T I S
C H O R E █ S H O D █ W E T █
```

32 MAKING FACES

```
J O S H █ R O T S █ P A S S
I D E A █ N I C H E █ A S A P
M E W L █ O S H E A █ L I V E
█ █ F I V E O ⏱ S H A D O W
█ █ A T T A █ O A T E R S █
A ⏱ W O R K O R A N G E █
M E A N Y █ R O M E █ P O T
E D I E █ E E L E R █ M I M I
B I T S █ T I L L S █ E X A M
A N S █ C D I I █ Z A I R E
█ C L E A N E D O N E S ⏱
A L B E I T █ R O D S █ █
C O U N T E R ⏱ W I S E █
U R L S █ R U E H L █ R E A L
R A G U █ A B R I L █ E A S Y
A X E S █ S Y S T █ D U K E
```

42 ALTERNATE SPELLING

```
S A B R E █ C D S █ G C L E F
A B O U T █ A R I █ E L I D E
L A T E R I S E R █ T O K E N
E C O █ A N T S █ M A V E N S
M I X E D M E S S A G E S █ █
█ █ B E A █ P A R █ A C T █
E A S E █ T Y P O █ I G L O O
M B A R K E E A U K P U O P R
M U L T I █ A T T N █ E T A T
A T E █ L B S █ █ A B S █
█ S P L I T D E C I S I O N
W I S E T O █ O A K S █ M A E
E N L A I █ F I R S T R A T E
P R I S M █ A L L █ R A G E D
T E P E E █ N Y S █ O M E N S
```

The alternating letters of 39-Across spell
MAKE UP OR BREAK UP.

51 THEMELESS 22

```
O H G O S H ■ ■ D O G S A G E
N A R N I A ■ F A L L S F O R
S L E A Z Y ■ I N D E N T E D
I L E N E ■ L T G E N ■ E S O
T E N D ■ D I N E R ■ E R I C
E Y E O P E N E R ■ D I D N T
■ ■ G N O M E S ■ B E N I T O
J A G ■ M O N S T E R ■ N O R
U N S E E N ■ C O N M E N ■ ■
S N A P S ■ L E N D A N E A R
T O N I ■ S I N G S ■ C R U E
M U D ■ S W A T S ■ T O M B A
I N H U M A N E ■ Z O D I A C
S C A P U L A R ■ A R E N D T
S E M I T E S ■ ■ P A S T E S
```

59 LIFE GETS IN THE WAY

```
M A C S ■ ■ G R A B ■ A P P S
E P E E S ■ R I C E ■ T R O T
S P I R E ■ A F T E R W O R K
H A L F T I M E ■ ■ C A C T I
U R I ■ T V S ■ Q U A R T E T
G E N T L Y ■ B U N S ■ O N T
A L G A E ■ P A I D ■ A R T S
■ ■ ■ T R U E S T O R Y ■ ■ ■
M A S S ■ K N E E ■ Y E A R S
E L M ■ L E N S ■ D E S R E E
G L U C O S E ■ J I B ■ M B A
A R G O T ■ ■ L O V E B O A T
H I G H S T Y L E ■ E L I T E
I S L E ■ B O D Y ■ R A R E R
T E E N ■ S U S S ■ ■ B E S S
```

67 THEMELESS 29

```
P O D C A S T ■ T H E J E R K
A L R O K E R ■ R E A L M E N
R E S P I R E ■ E N R O U T E
A S E ■ N U M B E R S ■ L O S
S T U D ■ M O R T Y ■ J A R S
O R S O N ■ R O O ■ B E T T E
L A S S I E S ■ P O O R E S T
■ ■ ■ H O W ■ ■ ■ A R I ■ ■ ■
S T R O B E S ■ C R I C K E T
C R E T E ■ E T A ■ S H A L E
R A M S ■ A L A R M ■ O R A L
A L I ■ S T L U C I A ■ A I L
T A X B A S E ■ A L L G O N E
C L E A N E R ■ S N E A K E R
H A D A G A S ■ S E X L E S S
```

75 THEMELESS 33

```
W I T H A S M I L E ■ B A C H
I N H A R M O N I C ■ I T A R
S T A R G A Z I N G ■ L I M O
C O N S U L A T E ■ G A M E S
■ ■ ■ H E L M S ■ V O T E R S
N I C ■ D E B ■ W I R E T A P
E N O S ■ R I G A M A R O L E
W H U P S ■ Q T Y ■ N A D E R
T I N A L O U I S E ■ L I N O
O B T R U D E ■ T A V ■ E S T
N I N E R S ■ C A R E S ■ ■ ■
S T O P S ■ S I T A T H O M E
L I S A ■ M I N I C O O P E R
A V E R ■ I N C O H E R E N T
W E S T ■ I N O N E S E N S E
```

13 THEMELESS 3

```
WITCHY   ABOMBS
ONEHOUR  RAGOUT
WATERLOO MEDUSA
 SEAM BRA ZESTY
STATEMOTTO NESS
TUT LUTHERAN
OPED MIO AGASSI
MOTOR CDV ASWAN
PRENUP OIL HEMP
 BRONXZOO EMU
SEGA RAJQUARTET
OXEYE PEU KOLN
FATLIP WELLTODO
ALGORE LIEOVER
STORER TYRESE
```

23 THEMELESS 8

```
STD PLASTIC MOM
CRI LALOOSH ALI
OUAGADOUGOU NIX
REMONSTRANT AVE
CLETE EISNER
HOTORCOLD SOARS
EVEN OBLASTS
DER CLEAVES EMP
 CREAMER AXER
PREXY HASITMADE
FOXCUB OPCIT
IMP NONONANETTE
ZEE CYCLOPEDIAS
ERR LEAGUER OTT
ROT ERRANDS NES
```

33 THEMELESS 13

```
MELANITES ZIPUP
OXYGENATE ECONO
PARACHUTE RESTS
SMARTENUP OSSIE
 ART SHEKELS
SORARE ASA
ELOI SLOWWITTED
WEARS BRA NERVE
NONSUBJECT REEF
 ESQ ABSENT
THORPES SNL
HERVE THEGAZEBO
RABIN ROLEMODEL
EPICS OPENENDED
ESTEE MISTREATS
```

43 THEMELESS 18

```
ETHANS JAPANESE
CHARON EVAPERON
HECUBA LIVEWIRE
ODIN FALSER CAM
IRE BUOYED MARY
SENTA RRS DOSE
MADEUPTO EAR
 MAXBIALYSTOCK
 ALP LOSESOUT
PANE AMU RETRY
TANS GROVES TOP
ORG FAIRER ROSE
PIECRUST REINAS
PALOALTO ONETWO
SHORTTON RELOAN
```

52 "ACHTUNG, BABY!"

M	I	D	D	L	E	■	■	R	A	T	E	D	P	G
I	B	E	R	I	A	■	■	I	N	U	T	E	R	O
L	A	M	E	N	T	■	■	V	O	N	N	E	G	U	T
D	R	O	I	D	S	■	I	R	A	N	■	A	D	O
■	■	M	A	U	L	E	D	■	E	S	S	E	N	■
M	I	R	A	■	P	A	R	A	B	L	E	■	■	■
A	D	O	R	E	■	N	O	N	O	■	C	R	U	Z
M	E	A	T	L	O	A	F	■	W	A	H	I	N	E
M	A	R	I	O	N	■	F	I	L	M	S	E	T	S
A	S	S	N	■	C	A	L	C	■	S	P	L	I	T
■	■	■	I	S	E	E	Y	O	U	■	I	S	L	A
E	R	A	S	E	■	R	I	N	S	E	S	■	■	■
R	A	P	■	L	O	I	N	■	A	U	T	H	O	R
I	N	T	H	E	B	A	G	■	B	R	O	O	K	E
C	O	L	O	N	E	L	■	■	L	O	L	L	E	D
A	N	Y	W	A	Y	S	■	■	E	S	S	A	Y	S

60 THEMELESS 26

A	S	L	A	N	T	■	■	B	A	D	S	A	N	T	A
B	M	I	N	O	R	■	■	B	L	E	E	P	E	R	S
F	I	B	O	N	A	C	C	I	S	E	R	I	E	S	■
A	R	E	■	O	N	E	■	N	E	D	■	L	E	T	■
B	K	L	Y	N	Q	N	S	E	X	P	W	Y	■	■	■
■	■	■	M	O	U	T	H	■	■	O	B	O	E	S	■
M	A	M	A	■	I	R	A	N	■	D	A	U	N	T	■
A	R	I	■	S	L	A	K	E	R	S	■	N	Y	U	■
S	C	R	A	M	■	L	I	T	E	■	E	G	A	D	■
K	O	A	L	A	■	■	R	I	V	A	L	■	■	■
■	■	B	I	L	L	M	A	Z	E	R	O	S	K	I	■
M	A	E	■	L	E	A	■	E	N	C	■	P	U	N	■
A	L	L	K	I	D	D	I	N	G	A	S	I	D	E	■
P	O	L	E	S	T	A	R	■	■	E	D	I	T	O	R
S	T	A	Y	H	O	M	E	■	■	D	E	T	E	S	T

68 SIGNS OF THE ...

F	A	T	A	L	■	D	C	V	■	B	A	R	E
A	R	O	M	A	■	I	R	E	■	E	N	I	D
M	A	N	Y	×	O	V	E	R	■	H	I	G	H	×
I	B	I	S	■	M	E	D	I	C	I	■	A	A	H
S	I	E	■	B	R	I	T	O	N	■	T	R	E
H	A	R	D	×	■	S	T	A	N	D	■	O	R	E
■	■	■	R	I	L	E	■	S	I	T	O	N	I	T
■	S	I	N	G	E	■	■	C	H	R	I	S	■
S	A	R	O	N	G	S	■	A	S	E	A	■	■
O	L	A	■	A	I	M	A	T	■	×	L	O	T	S
M	I	L	■	T	O	A	T	E	E	■	N	E	A
E	V	E	■	U	N	S	E	A	L	■	E	E	K	S
×	A	V	E	R	■	H	A	L	F	×	H	O	W	S
■	T	I	L	E	■	E	M	O	■	U	L	N	A	E
■	E	N	O	S	■	D	S	T	■	P	E	E	R	S

76 ZOUNDS!

P	O	O	P	■	■	A	B	B	R	■	B	I	A	S
S	P	A	R	K	■	R	E	L	O	■	E	N	Z	O
T	E	H	E	E	■	G	A	I	N	■	Q	T	I	P
■	■	R	U	N	A	R	O	U	N	D	S	U	E	Z
■	■	■	U	N	E	■	■	T	O	W	E	R	■	■
■	P	O	P	U	P	A	D	Z	■	I	S	L	A	M
C	O	B	S	■	A	V	E	■	U	T	T	E	R	S
E	L	F	■	B	I	G	B	E	N	Z	■	A	R	G
C	O	U	G	A	R	■	R	O	I	■	I	V	O	R
E	S	S	E	N	■	S	A	N	T	A	F	E	Z	■
■	■	C	A	D	R	E	■	■	A	L	F	■	■
■	B	A	R	B	E	C	U	E	S	P	I	T	Z	■
B	A	T	S	■	V	E	R	Y	■	H	E	R	O	D
B	L	E	U	■	E	D	G	E	■	A	S	A	N	A
L	I	S	P	■	L	E	E	S	■	■	T	M	E	N

14 SET 'EM UP

```
G E M   N C A A   L O G I C
E T O   A L U M   U P E N D
T A R O   N O D E   G E E K S
A L T H E A G I B S O N
T I E I N     A H S   S H E
  I M O L D F A S H I O N E D
    A O U T       T I R E
M A I D I N M A N H A T T A N
A R L O     L I E S
J A S O N A L E X A N D E R
A L A   O W E     E A M E S
    S T E V E M A R T I N I
B Y W A Y   E L A N   A G O G
B O W I E   R A Z E     R I M
Q U I L T   S L E W   E R A
```

24 CROSS-REFERENCING

```
S T E W   A C T   G R E A T K
E A C H   S E A   R A V I N E
E L O I   S N L   O M E R T A
S E L L S A T C T I O N
      S T I R   R N S   W E D
P O S T A L   M A S   B A D E
O T T   M E S O N   T O P I C
P O R T P R I N C E H A I T I
S O A P S   M E E S E   T E D
I L I E   P I T   O N S I D E
N E T   A R A   S P C A
      G R A N D T H E F T T O
V I S I N G   Y E A   A T R A
P O T F E U   N A G   R E E F
S U B T L E   E L I   I N X S
```

34 BASEBALL FOR THE BIRDS

```
L O B B Y   C A P S   P R E
A C U R A   S A G E T   R E D
S H R I K E T H R E E   E R G
S O N G   M Y N A L E A G U E
      H O M E     L I O N S
A R E T H A   N I X E D
S E T O N   N O M E   B A A
T E R N O N A F A S T B A L L
A L E   F L A X   E E R I E
    A F L A T   A R A B I C
O M A R R     A S I N
B O O B Y B O N D S   P S A T
G R R   P I G E O N C O A C H
Y E T   A T L A S   A L L I E
N S A   N E E R   N E E D Y
```

44 RR XING

```
J E T B L U E     D A N A
C L U E I N G   S H I I T E S
T O B A C C O   L I O N E T S
      K E A   T O R N D O W N
O A R S   S H O T S H I F T
S N O B   H E P   C O N
C O T E   E R I C H S   C A W
A R I A   D E C O   E M O T E
R A N D D   T A U S   A M T S
S K I   A D O L P H   I B I S
    O F O   B O A   N E R O
  F I S T S T I N G   E D E N
M E D I C A I D   G M C
A V E R A G E   L I M O G E S
R E S I D E D   T E M P U R A
C R T S     D R I S T A N
```

53 THEMELESS 23

```
H O M E L E S S S H E L T E R
I A M L E D T O B E L I E V E
T H E L A T E L A M E N T E D
S U S A N ■ ■ ■ ■ ■ I C E R S
■ ■ ■ ■ E A R L A P S ■ ■ ■ ■
C L A S S R O O M R O S T E R
H I G H T E N S I O N W I R E
E S A I ■ ■ ■ ■ ■ ■ ■ A N N S
F L I E S A T H A L F M A S T
S E N S A T I O N A L I S T S
■ ■ ■ ■ L E T I T G O ■ ■ ■ ■
P A S T A ■ ■ ■ ■ ■ R I O D E
S T E A M B O A T W I L L I E
I T A L I A N D R E S S I N G
S A L E S A S S I S T A N T S
```

61 DECISION MAKERS

```
F E Z ■ E M M A ■ O R A L B
I D O ■ M O O N ■ S O L A R A
G I N S B U R G ■ T O I L E S
S T E V E N S ■ ■ S T A Y S
■ ■ U D D E R ■ S T O L E N
A S H ■ ■ L O D E ■ ■ A R S
T H O M A S ■ B O X E S ■
T H E S U P R E M E C O U R T
■ S K I E R ■ S O U T E R
M S T ■ C I T Y ■ ■ A M Y
I C I C L E ■ S A W I I
L A T H E ■ ■ K E N N E D Y
A L A I N S J U S T I C E S
N I N E T Y E Z E R ■ H E E
■ A S F O R T A R O O R R
```

69 THEMELESS 30

```
P E T E B E S T ■ O S T A R S
A V E M A R I A ■ P E E L U P
R E T U R N T O ■ E L A I N E
■ ■ ■ T E E ■ V N E C K E D
T O P L E S S B E A C H E S ■
A R R A N T ■ A T I T ■ ■
S K I N D O C T O R ■ S A A B
T I M E S ■ L G E ■ O U T I E
E N O S ■ M A I D E N N A M E
■ ■ S O I R ■ S E U R A T
■ B O T T O M L E S S P I T S
B A R R O N S ■ L E I ■ ■
O N L I N E ■ R A N D O L P H
S T O K E R ■ E T C E T E R A
S U P E R S ■ W E E D B G O N
```

77 THEMELESS 34

```
C O N J U R O R ■ A C C U S E
A L O E V E R A ■ T O R N U P
M I S T U N E D ■ P L A T E S
O N E ■ L O G ■ P L A C I D O
■ ■ J A V A S E A ■ K E E N
A R E A ■ A N A L Y Z E ■ ■
C U R B S T O N E ■ O R D E R
H E R B I E ■ ■ J O J O B A
E S S E N ■ U R S A M A J O R
■ ■ R E C R O O M ■ C O N E
F L A W ■ R A T P A C K ■ ■
A E R O S O L ■ R I O ■ T R I
L A N C E S ■ M A C M A H O N
S N A K E S ■ O N A B R E A K
E N Z Y M E ■ M O N O T O N Y
```

15 THEMELESS 4

M	A	P	S	■	A	H	E	M	■	I	N	C	O	G
A	P	E	S	■	L	O	G	O	■	S	O	L	A	R
C	A	R	R	O	T	T	O	P	■	A	N	I	T	A
A	C	T	■	V	E	T	■	■	B	I	O	P	S	Y
W	H	I	T	E	R	U	S	S	I	A	N	■	■	■
S	E	N	O	R	■	B	E	A	S	H	A	M	E	D
■	■	E	N	D	S	■	C	R	T	■	N	A	M	E
C	A	N	Y	O	U	H	E	A	R	M	E	N	O	W
A	B	C	S	■	R	I	D	■	O	A	T	H	■	■
B	A	Y	O	N	E	T	E	D	■	S	T	A	S	H
■	■	P	A	S	S	S	E	N	T	E	N	C	E	■
E	S	P	R	I	T	■	■	C	O	E	■	D	A	R
M	O	R	A	L	■	Q	U	A	D	R	I	L	L	E
M	A	I	N	E	■	E	R	N	O	■	V	E	E	S
A	R	M	O	R	■	D	I	T	Z	■	E	D	D	Y

25 THEMELESS 9

A	G	R	E	E	T	O	■	P	A	T	C	A	S	H
W	H	O	K	N	E	W	■	A	R	I	O	S	T	O
G	E	N	E	R	A	L	E	L	E	C	T	I	O	N
E	N	C	■	I	B	E	A	M	■	■	T	A	W	■
E	T	O	■	C	A	T	S	P	A	J	A	M	A	S
■	■	B	O	G	■	T	I	L	E	■	I	W	O	■
A	L	L	■	S	A	L	L	I	E	■	N	A	N	■
O	B	I	T	S	■	L	A	O	■	P	L	O	Y	S
L	O	T	■	P	L	A	N	T	S	■	I	R	S	■
A	L	T	■	E	O	N	S	■	T	S	P	■	■	■
F	I	L	E	C	A	B	I	N	E	T	■	B	A	N
■	S	E	L	■	A	N	E	R	A	■	O	R	E	■
T	H	E	L	A	S	T	G	A	N	G	S	T	E	R
S	E	V	I	L	L	E	■	T	E	E	T	H	E	D
E	R	A	S	E	R	S	■	O	R	D	E	A	L	S

35 THEMELESS 14

P	E	N	P	A	L	S	■	C	A	R	C	A	R	E
D	R	I	E	D	U	P	■	O	N	E	O	V	E	R
T	A	X	R	A	T	E	■	F	T	B	R	A	G	G
■	■	■	S	P	E	C	I	F	I	E	D	■	■	■
R	O	B	O	T	■	I	L	E	■	L	O	G	I	N
A	N	O	N	■	P	A	L	E	R	■	N	I	C	E
N	E	D	■	R	E	L	A	T	E	R	■	V	E	X
P	A	Y	■	I	S	I	T	A	G	O	■	E	M	T
A	R	B	■	G	O	N	E	B	A	D	■	S	I	D
S	T	A	Y	■	S	T	A	L	L	■	M	I	L	A
T	H	R	E	W	■	E	S	E	■	G	U	N	K	Y
■	■	■	S	H	O	R	E	B	I	R	D	■	■	■
B	A	S	S	A	L	E	■	O	N	A	D	A	T	E
L	A	T	I	M	E	S	■	O	R	D	E	R	I	N
T	A	P	R	O	O	T	■	K	E	Y	R	I	N	G

45 THEMELESS 19

A	B	C	S	P	O	R	T	S	■	C	R	A	M	P
T	I	E	S	O	N	E	O	N	■	O	I	L	E	R
M	O	O	N	S	H	I	N	E	■	U	N	I	T	Y
■	■	■	■	T	I	N	G	L	I	N	G	■	■	■
R	A	T	E	D	G	■	S	L	A	T	I	N	G	S
A	R	A	P	A	H	O	■	■	G	E	N	E	R	A
G	S	U	I	T	■	R	A	Z	O	R	■	T	O	L
T	E	N	S	E	■	E	W	E	■	B	F	L	A	T
O	N	T	■	D	R	O	L	L	■	A	L	I	N	E
P	I	E	R	C	E	■	■	L	A	L	A	K	E	R
S	O	R	E	H	E	A	D	■	L	A	G	E	R	S
■	■	■	L	E	S	B	R	O	W	N	■	■	■	■
L	I	L	A	C	■	H	O	P	E	C	H	E	S	T
O	R	E	C	K	■	O	N	E	S	E	A	T	E	R
X	A	X	E	S	■	R	E	S	T	S	T	O	P	S

54 WHAT THE ELL?

Q	T	I	P	S	■	A	C	C	T	■	O	D	D	S
B	Y	N	O	W	■	B	A	L	I	■	L	E	A	P
E	L	A	T	E	ELL	F	O	R	A	D	A	N	O	
R	E	N	T	A	L	■	E	V	E	N	■	T	E	T
T	R	E	E	T	O	P	■	E	D	I	T	H		
■	■	R	E	C	E	S	S	■	T	O	B	E		
S	R	I	■	R	U	S	H	■	S	A	U	L	B	ELL
M	O	N	A	■	S	T	ELL	A	C	■	T	O	R	O
ELL	S	A	R	A	T	■	A	M	O	S	■	W	O	W
■	E	M	I	L	■	T	R	I	P	U	P			
■	A	D	O	B	E	■	D	E	B	A	T	E	S	
S	A	N	■	H	O	N	E	■	D	U	P	O	N	T
P	E	N	N	A	N	D	T	ELL	■	R	U	N	T	Y
A	R	E	A	■	E	T	T	E	■	B	A	G	E	L
M	O	R	T	■	S	O	U	R	■	S	N	A	R	E

62 TWO BITS

G	E	A	R	■	A	S	K	E	W	■	J	U	M	P
L	U	K	E	■	R	E	E	V	E	■	E	Z	I	O
A	R	I	D	■	T	H	R	E	E	¼	T	I	M	E
D	O	N	A	T	I	O	N	S	■	R	E	S	E	T
■	■	■	L	E	E	R	■	■	P	E	R			
¼	L	Y	E	A	R	N	I	N	G	S	■	C	H	I
D	O	E	R	■	■	N	E	A	T	■	R	I	P	
E	T	A	T	S	■	C	F	O	■	S	I	E	N	A
C	T	R	■	T	S	A	R	■	N	E	D	S		
K	O	S	■	N	A	V	A	L	H	E	A	D	¼	S
■	■	N	I	X	■	O	A	K	S					
A	T	T	I	C	■	I	N	C	R	E	M	E	N	T
¼	B	A	C	K	S	N	E	A	K	■	U	S	E	R
O	A	T	H	■	S	K	A	T	E	■	C	A	S	E
F	R	E	E	■	T	Y	P	E	D	■	H	U	S	K

70 THE GRAVITY OF THE SITUATION

D	R	A	B	■	A	L	I	S	T	■	A	M	F	M
A	O	N	E	■	C	A	N	O	E	■	F	A	L	A
T	A	K	E	L	E	T	T	U	C	E	F	R	O	M
A	M	A	R	E	T	T	O	■	U	N	R	I	P	E
■	■	■	B	Y	E	■	I	M	E	A	N			
P	O	S	T	A	L	■	R	R	S	■	Y	A	M	S
A	S	T	O	N	■	B	A	A	E	D	■	T	E	E
T	H	E	T	O	P	O	F	T	H	E	P	I	L	E
H	E	P	■	N	O	L	T	E	■	C	A	N	E	D
S	A	F	E	■	N	O	S	■	B	I	N	G	E	S
■	■	A	N	T	I	S	■	D	A	B				
S	E	T	T	E	E	■	T	E	L	E	T	Y	P	E
O	R	H	E	A	D	S	W	I	L	L	R	O	L	L
P	I	E	R	■	U	T	I	C	A	■	E	G	O	S
H	E	R	S	■	P	A	G	E	D	■	K	A	T	E

78 OPENING PAIR

X	E	R	S	■	V	O	W	■	A	S	T	R	O	
X	R	A	Y	S	■	I	N	A	■	S	T	E	E	D
L	A	Y	R	E	A	D	E	R	■	P	A	N	S	Y
■	S	K	I	A	R	E	A	■	H	E	I	S	T	S
A	U	R	A	■	C	O	M	E	A	C	R	O	S	S
D	R	O	N	E	S	■	■	L	I	T	■	R	U	E
D	E	C	A	L	■	F	O	R	K	■	S	P	Y	
■	■	■	I	N	O	R	O	U	T					
A	M	A	■	I	N	K	Y	■	A	L	E	R	T	
T	I	S	■	M	C	D	■	P	R	A	Y	E	R	
T	A	K	E	C	H	A	R	G	E	■	N	E	V	E
I	S	O	L	D	E	■	E	A	R	A	C	H	E	
R	A	V	E	L	■	S	E	T	T	H	E	O	R	Y
E	R	E	C	T	■	A	V	E	■	A	R	O	S	E
D	A	R	T	S	■	Y	E	S	■	■	S	K	E	W

16 THREE IN A ROW

S	A	R	A	H	■	■	O	T	C	■	B	E	L	A
E	V	I	T	A	■	O	N	E	I	■	A	X	E	L
C	A	S	E	W	O	R	K	E	R	■	F	I	X	E
T	S	K	■	A	T	I	P	■	R	E	F	L	U	X
S	T	Y	M	I	E	■	■	D	U	L	L	E	S	■
■	■	A	I	R	■	A	I	S	L	E	■	■	■	■
X	M	A	S	■	I	S	N	T	■	A	M	O	R	E
E	X	I	S	T	■	TIC	TAC	TOE	■	S	E	W	O	N
S	I	X	T	H	■	K	I	D	S	■	N	E	M	O
■	■	R	E	W	E	D	■	I	N	T	■	■	■	■
■	S	H	A	M	I	R	■	■	L	E	S	S	E	N
O	P	I	N	E	S	■	D	R	E	W	■	H	R	E
P	O	T	S	■	P	R	E	E	X	A	M	I	N	E
T	R	O	I	■	E	A	U	X	■	R	A	P	I	D
S	E	N	T	■	■	D	I	X	■	■	K	E	S	E	Y

26 SÍ FOOD

H	A	S	T	A	■	B	A	R	N	■	F	L	I	P
A	L	T	A	R	■	E	R	I	E	■	R	E	N	O
L	I	E	U	T	■	D	E	F	I	C	I	E	N	T
T	O	R	T	I	L	L	A	F	L	A	T	■	■	■
S	T	E	■	S	E	A	■	■	N	O	W	A	Y	■
■	■	H	O	T	T	A	M	A	L	E	S	■	I	L	E
■	■	S	I	R	■	M	A	V	■	B	L	O	W	■
H	O	L	Y	G	U	A	C	A	M	O	L	E	■	■
S	O	U	L	■	I	R	S	■	■	O	O	F	■	■
U	P	N	■	S	A	L	S	A	M	U	S	I	C	■
V	I	D	E	O	■	■	L	P	S	■	N	I	B	■
■	■	■	B	I	G	E	N	C	H	I	L	A	D	A
N	O	V	E	L	I	D	E	A	■	E	I	N	E	S
O	D	O	R	■	G	I	M	P	■	S	A	C	R	E
T	E	X	T	■	S	T	O	P	■	T	R	E	S	S

36 QUARTERLY BRIEFS

T	S	A	R	S	■	B	A	J	A	■	C	O	M	■
A	T	S	E	A	■	A	W	E	S	■	O	R	E	M
P	R	I	M	R	O	SEP	A	T	H	■	N	A	N	A
P	I	N	■	A	P	A	R	T	■	A	C	T	O	R
E	D	I	T	■	A	Y	E	■	P	R	OCT	O	R	S
D	E	N	I	A	L	■	L	E	G	■	R	A	H	■
■	S	E	E	S	■	C	S	I	N	Y	■	S	H	Y
■	■	S	H	O	R	T	F	A	L	L	■	■	■	■
A	P	T	■	A	D	O	P	T	■	E	A	S	T	■
Z	O	E	■	M	O	P	■	A	S	I	T	I	S	■
T	U	R	NOV	E	R	■	F	S	U	■	R	U	T	H
E	R	R	E	D	■	F	L	I	T	S	■	N	A	T
C	O	I	L	■	E	A	U	DEC	O	L	O	G	N	E
S	U	E	T	■	E	M	M	A	■	I	N	U	I	T
■	T	R	Y	■	L	E	E	R	■	P	E	N	A	L

46 SEEING THE SITES

E	L	E	C	T	S	■	P	A	P	P	■	S	E	W
G	A	L	O	O	T	■	A	R	I	A	■	E	T	A
G	I	L	A	M	O	N	S	T	E	R	■	W	A	Y
O	R	A	L	■	R	U	T	S	■	T	W	A	I	N
■	■	■	B	A	R	N	E	Y	G	O	O	G	L	E
L	O	G	I	N	S	■	■	O	N	M	E	■	■	■
U	P	E	N	D	■	S	L	A	T	E	B	L	U	E
S	I	T	■	P	O	U	C	H	■	■	I	S	O	■
T	E	S	T	M	A	T	C	H	■	L	I	N	E	N
■	■	T	O	O	T	■	■	N	I	N	E	R	S	■
Y	A	H	O	O	S	E	R	I	O	U	S	■	■	■
O	D	E	L	L	■	R	A	P	T	■	P	E	R	U
U	M	A	■	A	M	A	Z	O	N	R	I	V	E	R
V	E	X	■	H	O	S	E	■	O	B	R	I	E	N
E	N	E	■	S	P	E	D	■	W	I	E	L	D	S